Making Decorative *Fabric Covered* BOXES

Making Decorative Fabric Covered Boxes

Mary Jo Hiney

Sterling Publishing Co., Inc. New York

A Sterling/Chapelle Book

For Chapelle Limited

Owner
Jo Packham

Editor
Amanda McPeck

Artwork
Sally Vedder-Morley

Staff:
Malissa Boatwright
Sara Casperson
Rebecca Christensen
Amber Hansen
Holly Hollingsworth
Susan Jorgensen
Susan Laws
Barbara Milburn
Pat Pearson
Leslie Ridenour
Cindy Rooks
Cindy Stoeckl
Ryanne Webster
Nancy Whitley

Photography:
Kevin Dilley for Hazen
    Photography

Photography Styling:
Cherri Herrick
Susan Laws

Special Thanks to:
Ann Winn, for her porcelain doll
  used in photography.
Josh and Alexis Hiney, for their
  help in making patterns.

If you have any questions or
comments or would like in-
formation on specialty prod-
ucts featured in this book,
please contact:
Chapelle Ltd., Inc.
PO Box 9252
Ogden, UT 84409
(801) 621-2777
(801) 621-2788 (fax)

Library of Congress Cataloging-in-Publication Data

Hiney, Mary Jo
  Making decorative fabric covered boxes / Mary Jo Hiney
        p.   cm.
  "A Sterling/Chapelle book."
  Includes index.
  ISBN 0-8069-1296-0
  1. Box making. 2. Box craft. 3. Ornamental boxes. 4. Textile fabrics. I. Title
  TT870.5.H49   1996
  745.593--dc20   95-37036

10 9 8 7 6 5 4 3

Published by Sterling Publishing Company, Inc.
387 Park Avenue South, New York, N.Y. 10016
©1996 by Chapelle Limited
Distributed in Canada by Sterling Publishing c/o Canadian Manda Group, One Atlantic Avenue,
  Suite 105, Toronto, Ontario, Canada M6K 3E7
Distributed in Great Britain and Europe by Cassell PLC, Wellington House, 125 Strand, London
  WC2R 0BB, England
Distributed in Australia by Capricorn Link (Australia) Pty Ltd. P.O. Box 6651, Baulkham Hills,
  Business Centre, NSW 2153, Australia

Printed in Hong Kong
Sterling ISBN 0-8069-1296-0

Contents

To Family

To the gift my husband and children are to me
To my family of origin, a family that has had the courage to confront difficult issues.

I'm proud of my blue collar roots–they are the solid foundation of my life. I've learned a lot from watching my family work.

My father was a gifted cabinetmaker with superior skills and workmanship. He felt strongly that it was his responsibility to care for the financial needs of his family. Because he had old-fashioned values, he was not comfortable with letting my mom work outside the home. Even though it's been 13 years since my dad left this earth, he is still taking care of my mom. In my opinion, that's an awesome accomplishment for a man who had only a third-grade education.

To earn extra money, Dad took on side jobs that he assembled in our garage. Seeing him work taught me the wonders of completion and ingenuity. Although cabinets were his specialty, he built some entirely unrelated things in that garage as well. The year I was a senior in high school, he built a 5-foot-tall knight in shining armor. Our school football team was called the Valiants, and a knight in full armor was our mascot. Today, 20 years later, that replica still stands in the school library. At times our efforts feel small. Over the years, and possibly unknown to us, their impact can be seen and felt, and they are not in vain.

I can see quite a legacy in the efforts left by a simple man.

We didn't have a lot of spare money when I was a kid. Whenever she could save a few dollars from her grocery money, Mom would purchase fabric, 3 yards for a dollar. Once I learned to sew, I was hooked. Rather than going to the fabric store to buy a piece of fabric for a project I had in mind, I shopped in Mom's fabric drawers. My creativity was greatly enhanced by that lack of spare money. To this day, I can make something from thin air and a few scraps of fabric.

For a period of time, I had the opportunity to work with another master cabinetmaker, my little brother. Frank taught me valuable skills that helped improve and perfect my box making ability.

Just recently, my older brother Ric began making furniture. I'm sure that seeds of interest were planted in early childhood. Often, Dad would give him a piece of wood and a box of nails. Ric would spend hours happily pounding every nail straight into that little block of wood. Today, he is a meticulous worker, entrusted with difficult projects.

Making boxes from cardboard makes me feel like a cabinetmaker, and I work in my garage as well. That's my room. Lot's of things emerge from there in a completed stage. My boxes stay with me briefly, and then they're gone and I never see them again. If my kids remember beautiful fineries emerging from the garage, I'd like that very much.

A Box Story

Sarah was an 11-year-old orphan who lived with her aunt, a bitter middle-aged woman who was greatly annoyed with the burden of caring for her sister's daughter. She never failed to remind young Sarah that if it had not been for her generosity, she would be in an orphanage. Still, with all of the scolding and with all of the rejection at home, Sarah was a sweet and gentle child.

Her teacher, Ms. Williams had not noticed Sarah much until she began staying after school each day (at the risk of arousing her aunt's anger) to help her straighten up the classroom. They worked quietly and comfortably, not speaking much, but sharing the solitude of that hour of the day. When they did talk, Sarah spoke mostly of her mother. Though Sarah was quite young when her mother died, she remembered a kind, gentle, loving woman who always spent time with her.

As Christmas drew nearer, however, Sarah failed to stay after school each day. Ms. Williams looked forward to her coming, but as the days passed, she continued to scamper hurriedly from the room after class. One afternoon, Ms. Williams asked her why she no longer helped her in the classroom. She told her how much she missed her, and Sarah's large grey eyes lit up eagerly as she replied, "Did you really miss me?" Ms. Williams said Sarah was her best helper. "I am making you a surprise," Sarah whispered confidentially. "It's for Christmas." With that, she became embarrassed and dashed from the room.

The day before Christmas, Sarah crept slowly into the room late that afternoon, with her hands concealing something behind her back. "I have your present," she said timidly when Ms. Williams looked up. She held out her hands, and there in her tiny palms was a box.

"It's beautiful, Sarah. Is there something in it?" Ms. Williams asked.

"Yes," she replied, so Ms. Williams opened the top and looked inside. "Oh, you can't see what's in it," Sarah explained, "and you can't touch it, or taste it, or smell it, but my Mother always said it makes you feel good all of the time . . . warm on cold nights, and safe when you are alone."

Ms. Williams gazed into the empty box. "What is it, Sarah, that will make me feel so good?"

"It is love," she whispered, "and Mother always said it is best when you give it away." Then she turned and quietly left the room.

May all of your boxes be filled with love.

-M.J.

Box Making Basics

TOOLS AND MATERIALS

• **Before making a box, read both the Box Making Basics and the individual box instructions thoroughly and carefully.**

• Gather the materials and tools you need. Basic tools are listed in the box to the side. Additional tools and materials are listed in a box with the instructions for each box.

• Cut all fabric and cardboard. A chart for each box lists how many pieces of fabric and cardboard you need for each pattern piece. When the chart instructs you to add a certain amount to the pattern (e.g., + ¼"), add amount to all sides of pattern.

• Many patterns need to be enlarged on a photocopy machine. Patterns that give measurements (e.g., box sides) are best drawn by hand using a precise ruler.

Tools

For every box you make you need:

3"-wide paint roller
Tacky glue
Thin bodied tacky glue
Hot glue gun and glue sticks
Craft scissors
Fabric scissors
Dowels
Heavy and/or light-weight cardboard
Precise ruler
Utility knife
Pencil
Wet and dry rags
Brown paper bag

Paint Roller

A 3"-wide disposable paint roller (A) spreads glue onto cardboard surfaces just like a paint roller spreads paint onto a wall. It is a wonderful way to achieve thorough coverage of cardboard surfaces. The roller can be washed out with soap and water and reused for many projects.

Tacky Glue

In order to laminate fabric to cardboard, use **thin-bodied** tacky glue (A). It bonds fabric to cardboard without staining the fabric. It is the perfect consistency to paint onto cardboard, using a disposable paint roller. The laminating process is half the work and three times the bond when you use the right kind of tacky glue.

Hot Glue Gun and Glue Sticks

Hot glue (A) is the best glue for box construction. Use the "cloudy" glue stick (A). The clear sticks do not penetrate fabric well for a good bond, and the yellow ones are for surfaces like wood. Whenever hot glue is used, it must be flattened thoroughly so bulk is eliminated. *(Tacky glue can be used for box construction, but it needs to set up for each step and held together with clothespins or masking tape until dry.)*

Embellishment Glues

Trims can be applied to boxes with hot glue, but tacky glue is the best for gluing trims in place (A). It is also less tricky than hot glue, but it has to set up a minute or two first. Tacky glue can also bond brass, buttons and other similar surfaces to the fabric. However, for a better, and more permanent, bond for such items, use an industrial-strength adhesive.

Craft Scissors

Good craft scissors are essential in order to cut cardboard shapes accurately (B). Designate a pair of high-quality scissors for cardboard cutting. They have a very refined cutting edge, which makes it possible to get into tight areas, and they are very strong. If you are having difficulty cutting cardboard, the thickness of the blades could be causing the problem.

Fabric Scissors

Designate a special pair of scissors for cutting fabrics (B). Using your fabric scissors to cut other materials will dull the blades and make them less effective at cutting fabric.

A: Clockwise: Hot glue gun and glue sticks, Paint roller, and Tacky glue

Lightweight Cardboard

You can use railroad board, poster board, or chip board (c). The thinness of these boards makes the cardboard pliable. Railroad and poster board can be white on both sides, whereas chip board is grey. White board is preferred, as the grey board can discolor fabric.

Many stores order railroad board as their poster board. Railroad board has a dull finish; poster board has a shiny finish. It is best to use 8- or 10-ply railroad or poster board. Inquire at the store as to what ply has been ordered. In most cases, one half sheet can make many boxes. If only 6 ply is available, it can be used.

c: Clockwise: Metal ruler, Heavy cardboard, Labeled patterns, Lightweight cardboard, Utility knife

Dowels

Wooden dowels are used to shape box sides by rolling. Dowels 8"long and 1", ½" and ¼" wide (B) are enough to get any job done.

Heavy Cardboard

You can use crescent board, mat board, or process board (c). Heavy cardboard is 1/16" thick and sturdy, yet thin enough to be cut with scissors. It can be found at hobby stores and art supply stores. The board should be white on both sides. In most cases, one sheet can make many boxes. Process board is the best. 1/16"-thick chip board can be substituted if no other kind is available.

B: Clockwise: Disappearing pen, Craft scissors, 1", ½" and ¼" dowels, Fabric scissors

Ruler

A ruler with precise measurements (c) is essential for making perfect boxes. Yardsticks and cloth tape measures are not precise!

Utility Knife

Use a utility knife (c) to score the cardboard. It can also be used to cut some of the more difficult shapes if desired. Use caution and develop skill with this tool. Remember, a sharp blade is safer than a dull blade.

Pencil

Always keep your pencil as sharp as possible. When measuring, mark cardboard for box sides and scores with a dot at the precise mark to keep measurements accurate.

Rags

A wet rag and a dry rag are necessary to keep hands clean so fabric is not stained with glue.

Brown Paper Bag

An opened brown paper bag is perfect as a "drop cloth." Place cardboard parts onto paper while rolling with glue.

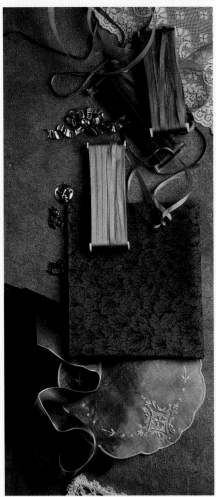

D: RIBBONS, LACES, CHARMS AND FABRICS

TECHNIQUES

Labeling

Label each piece of cardboard in a noticeable but not interfering location, like the center underside (C, see page 9). Label each piece of fabric with a piece of pinned paper. Label each piece immediately after cutting. Always keep fabrics and cardboard pieces together.

Plain or Fancy

Any fancy box can be made plain with little or no trims, and any plain box can be made fancy. The box patterns provided in this book are designed to work either way. Trims may be changed on any box. Be creative!

Surprise Fabric

The first thing anybody does when holding any kind of box is to look inside. Don't disappoint the beholder—choose an inside fabric that is a wonderful surprise!

Scoring

Place precision ruler onto score marks. Slice halfway through cardboard with utility knife at marks across width of cardboard. These are mountain scores (C, see page 9).

Valley scores are made on the opposite side of the cardboard. Mark location of score at top edge of cardboard side. Flip cardboard over and score (C). Remember to score cardboard before covering with fabric.

Fabric-Covering Tips

Boxes with inward curves or box insides that are covered with fabric must be laminated. A fabric that will not stain must be used. Most silks and lightweight polyesters will stain. Test by laminating onto cardboard scrap if there are any doubts.

The fabric covering process sets the stage for a better finished product. Be precise. At pointed parts of a shape, dab frays with extra glue and wrap frays onto wrong side of cardboard. At indented curves, use fingernail and extra dab of glue to further emphasize shape.

Laminating

Prepare a wet rag and a dry rag for constant hand cleaning. Place or tape brown paper bag onto work surface. Pour enough tacky glue into a disposable plastic or tin dish to cover bottom of dish. Place cardboard onto paper bag. Place fabric wrong side up on work surface.

Roll glue onto paint roller in dish. Completely cover roller's surface, then roll off extra glue in dish. Paint entire surface of cardboard with glue (1A). Make sure to follow any instructions regarding which side should be laminated if the cardboard is scored.

Place glued cardboard on fabric by flipping cardboard over onto wrong side of fabric and pressing in place (1B).

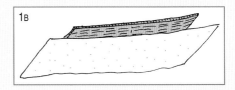

Flip fabric and cardboard over and smooth fabric completely. Eliminate any wrinkles immediately. Pay special attention to edges. Fabric should adhere to cardboard everywhere, especially at the edges (1C).

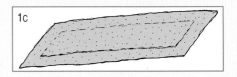

Turn laminated cardboard over again. Use roller to paint edges of cardboard and fabric with glue (1D).

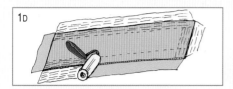

Trim out bulk from each corner, then wrap extended fabric over onto glued edges (1E).

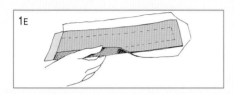

Double-check corners for fraying fabric, and dab frays with glue if necessary. Let dry for 10 minutes.

Most box sides will have one un-wrapped edge to be used as a tab to join the box sides together (1F).

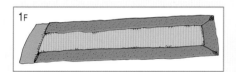

Wrap Method

Place fabric onto work surface, right side down. Center cardboard over fabric. Make sure to follow any instructions regarding which side should be wrapped if the cardboard is scored. Trim out bulk from any cor-

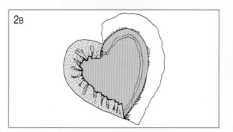

ners, then wrap edges of fabric over cardboard (2A and 2B).

Double-check corners for fraying fabric, and dab frays with glue if necessary. Let dry for 10 minutes.

Pad and Wrap

Lightly glue surface of cardboard shape. Place onto batting (3A).

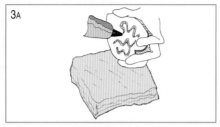

Trim batting flush to cardboard's edge, beveling scissors inward slightly (3B).

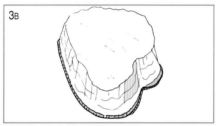

Place fabric wrong side up on work surface. Center padded cardboard over fabric (3C).

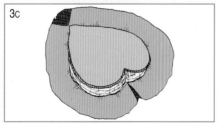

Glue 1" at inner edge of cardboard and wrap fabric onto glue. On opposite edge, glue and wrap another 1" worth of fabric onto cardboard. Pull fabric snugly.

Continue to glue and wrap fabric onto cardboard a small amount at a time, pulling the fabric as snugly as possible (3D). Exact shape of cardboard should not be altered when fabric is wrapped.

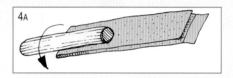

Rolling Cardboard with Dowel

Score lines are always emphasized after cardboard is covered and before cardboard is rolled. Do this by folding cardboard at score and rolling 1" dowel over fold (4A).

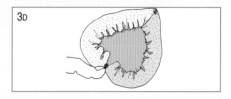

Some boxes have both mountain scores and valley scores. Make sure to fold scores on appropriate side.

Place cardboard on work surface, required side up. Place dowel at outer edge of cardboard. Begin to wrap cardboard around dowel without squaring off cardboard (4B).

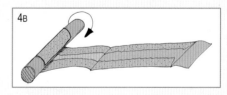

Continue to roll remaining length of cardboard as indicated in box directions (4C). Use inside bottom shape as a guide to mold cardboard.

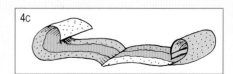

BOX CONSTRUCTION

Thickened-Lid-Style Boxes

This type of box is identical to hinge-lid-style boxes–without the hinges! The lid is removable, but the box side is not visually interrupted by a lid strip.

Hinge-Lid-Style Boxes

Assembling Box Bottom

Join short edges of box side by overlapping finished short edge to tab edge and butting cardboard edges up to each other. Glue tab in place (5A).

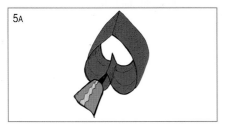

Working upside down, slip inside bottom shape into box bottom (5B).

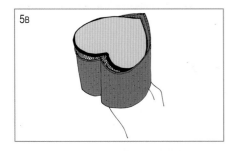

Secure with a thin bead of hot glue (5C).

Hold till dry. Continue to glue inside bottom shape to box side, about 1" at a time, until complete. Re-emphasize box's shape by molding with fingers.

Lining Strips

Finger-gather the lining fabric, right side up, onto strip while gluing in place. (An alternative is to gather-stitch around the outer edge of lining fabric, ⅛" from edge.) Adjust gathers to fit lining strip. Glue in place (6A).

When all fabric has been glued to strip, the strip becomes circular and inside out (6B).

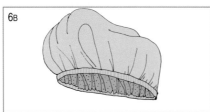

Cut a piece of batting to fit bottom of box, and place inside box (6C).

Flip lining strip, fabric right side out. Turn down cardboard strip so that lining has a finished edge (6D).

Keep ribbon hinges extended out from box. Glue wrong side of strip to inside of box side at top edge, thoroughly flattening glue. Begin gluing at center of the strip (6E). Where cardboard edges meet, you will be able to adjust lining strip larger or smaller as needed, depending on fabric weight.

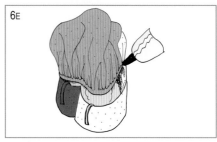

Gluing Ribbon Hinge to Inside Lid

Rest inside lid, right side down, into top edge of the box, and hold in place. Glue ribbon hinge(s) onto wrong side of inside lid, creating a snug fit. Center and glue wrong side of inside lid to right side of middle lid. Flatten glue thoroughly.

Flask- and Hidden-Lid-Strip-Style Boxes

Assembling Box Bottom

Snugly wrap inside box side around inside bottom. Hold in place and mark overlap. Overlap and glue one short edge of inside box side to opposite edge at mark (5A). Working upside down, slip inside box bottom into inside box side ⅟₁₆" down from box side's edge (5B). Glue in place (5C).

Glue outside box side to inside box side, wrong sides together (7A). Overlap and glue edges of outside box side to finish. Flatten glue thoroughly.

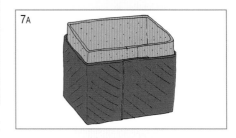

The inside box side stands taller than the outside box side of flask-style boxes. The reverse is true for hidden-lid-strip-style boxes.

Laminating Lid Strip

Place lid strip fabric wrong side up on work surface. Paint lid strip with laminating glue. Make sure to follow any instructions regarding which side should be down if the cardboard is scored. Place glued lid strip ¼" up from one long edge of fabric and centered between short edges. Flip fabric and cardboard over. Completely smooth fabric to cardboard. Be sure fabric is entirely adhered to all edges of cardboard. Trim off the ¼" excess fabric from bottom edge of cardboard (8A).

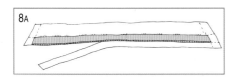

Place lid strip on work surface, uncovered side up. Glue ½" of one short edge of fabric. Wrap short edge over on itself at cardboard's edge (8B). Do not glue or cut remaining short edge of fabric.

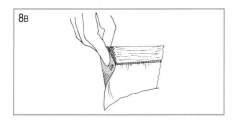

Paint uncovered lid strip with glue. Wrap upper fabric onto glued cardboard and smooth completely (8C).

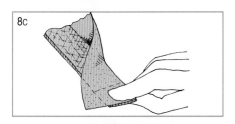

Lid strip is now completely covered with fabric and ½" of fabric extends past cardboard's long edge (8D).

Extended fabric side of cardboard is the outside of the lid strip. Let dry for 10 minutes.

Assembling Lid

Snugly wrap lid strip around inside lid. Hold in place and mark overlap, with finished edge outside. (Some lid strips butt together as in 5A). Overlap and glue finished short edge of lid strip to opposite edge at mark. Slip inside lid into lid strip at edge with extended fabric.

Glue extended fabric over onto wrong side of inside lid, pulling fabric tight for a snug fit (9A).

Continue to glue extended fabric of lid strip completely onto shape. Clip curves as necessary and thoroughly flatten glue.

EMBROIDERY WORK

Tracing

When tracing transfer diagrams onto fabric, use a disappearing pen. You do not have to transfer all marks–use them as a general placement guide.

Ribbon Tips

Always keep the ribbon loose and flat while working stitches. Untwist ribbon often and pull ribbon softly so it lies flat on top of fabric. Be creative with the stitching. Exact stitch placement is not critical, but make sure any placement marks are covered.

Needles

A size 3 crewel embroidery needle works well for most fabrics when using 4mm ribbon. For 7mm ribbon, use a chenille needle, sizes 18 to 24. As a rule of thumb, the barrel of the needle must create a hole large enough for the ribbon to pass through. If ribbon does not pull through fabric easily, a larger needle is needed.

To Thread Ribbon on Needle

(1) Thread the ribbon through the eye of the needle. With the tip of the needle, pierce the center of the ribbon ¼" from end.

(2) Pull remaining ribbon through to "lock" ribbon on needle.

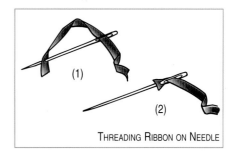

THREADING RIBBON ON NEEDLE

Knotting End of Ribbon

(1) Drape the ribbon in a circular manner to position the end of the ribbon perpendicular to the tip of the needle.

(2) Pierce the end of the ribbon with the needle, sliding the needle through the ribbon as if to make a short basting stitch.

(3) Pull needle and ribbon through the stitch portion to form a knot at end of ribbon.

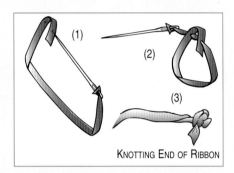

KNOTTING END OF RIBBON

To End Stitching

Secure stitches in place for each flower or small area. Do not drag the ribbon from one area to another. Tie a slip knot on the wrong side of needlework to secure the stitch in place and end ribbon.

Embroidery Stitches

Azalea

Mark five 2"-wide intervals on ribbon. Gather-stitch each interval with continuous stitches. Pull thread tightly to gather. Secure thread. Join last petal to first to hide raw edges.

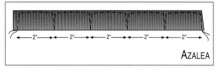

AZALEA

Beading Stitch

Using one strand of floss, come up through fabric. Slide the bead on the needle and push the needle back down through fabric. Knot off each bead or set of beads.

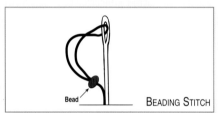

Bead

BEADING STITCH

Bullion Rose

(1) Come up at A and go down at B, leaving a loop. Come up again at A with the needle tip only. Wrap the loop thread around the needle tip until the twists equal the distance between A and B. Gently pull the needle through the twists, holding twists flat on the fabric with the needle. Insert needle again at B. This is a BULLION STITCH.

(2) Stitch 2 more BULLION STITCHES in the same shade.

(3) Stitch more BULLION STITCHES in different shades around previous BULLION STITCHES.

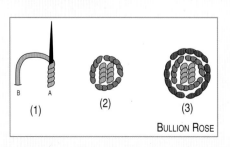

(1)   (2)   (3)

BULLION ROSE

Bullion Lazy Daisy

Complete as LAZY DAISY (see page 16), but tack with a bullion stitch.

(1) Bring the needle up at A. Keep the ribbon flat, untwisted and full. Put the needle down through fabric at B and up at C, but do not pull through.

(2) Snugly wrap ribbon around needle tip one to three times. Holding finger over wrapped ribbon, pull needle through ribbon. Take the needle back down into fabric at tip of bullion wraps, in direction stitch curves.

(3) Completed BULLION LAZY DAISY.

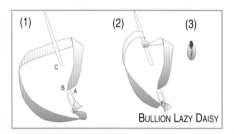

(1)   (2)   (3)

BULLION LAZY DAISY

Cascading Stitch

The CASCADING STITCH can be done starting with a bow or just using ribbon to cascade streamers through design. When starting with a bow, leave streamers long enough to work cascade through design. Thread streamer on needle, stitch down through fabric where bow placement is desired and come back up at start of cascade effect. This will hold the bow in place.

(1) Come up at A and go down at B. Come back up at C, allowing ribbon to twist and lay loosely on the fabric.

(2) Go down again at B and come up at C, making a small backstitch. This keeps the cascading in place.

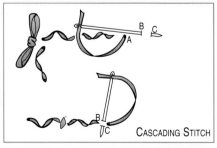

CASCADING STITCH

Couching Stitch

(1) Complete a straight stitch base by coming up at A and going down at B (the desired length of the straight stitch). Make sure the ribbon is flat and loose.

(2) Make a short tight straight stitch across the ribbon base to "couch" the straight stitch. Come up at C on one side of the ribbon. Go down at D on the opposite side of the ribbon. The tight, short stitch across the ribbon will cause the ribbon to gather and pucker. The straight stitch base is tacked at varying intervals.

(3) Completed COUCHING STITCH.

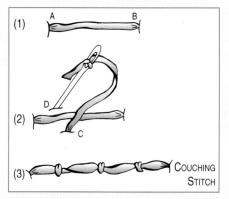

COUCHING STITCH

Dwarf Dahlia

(1) Make 5 folded petals. Pin to hold. Gather stitch ¼" from cut edges of ribbon, joining all 5 petals together in a chain.

(2) Pull thread as tight as possible to gather. Secure thread. Join last petal to first. Make a GRAPE for center of flower (see page 16).

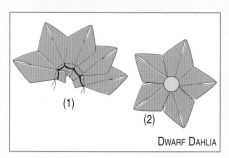

DWARF DAHLIA

Fluting

(1) Attach 1 ribbon end to fabric fold diagonally down and glue. Fold up and down diagonally again and glue. Repeat for entire area to be fluted. Fluting should extend ¼" past edge to be fluted.

(2) Competed FLUTING.

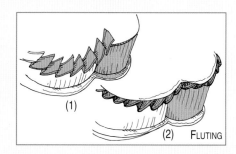

(2) FLUTING

Folded Petal and Leaf

Cut ribbon to desired length. Overlap ends of ribbon, and gather-stitch at bottom edge. Gather tightly. Wrap thread around stitches to secure. Trim excess ⅛" past stitching.

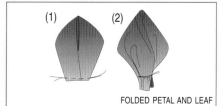

FOLDED PETAL AND LEAF

French Knot

(1) Bring needle up through fabric; smoothly wrap ribbon once around needle. (Ribbon can be wrapped 1-6 times around needle.)

(2) Hold ribbon securely off to one side, and push needle down through fabric at the starting point.

(3) Completed FRENCH KNOTS.

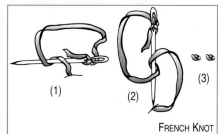

FRENCH KNOT

Gathered Leaf

(1) Fold ribbon in half, matching short ends. Turn folded ribbon corners ⅛" from top edge.

(2) Gather-stitch along edge. Pull to gather and secure thread. Open and shape leaf.

(3) Completed GATHERED LEAF.

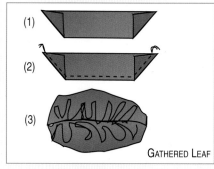

GATHERED LEAF

Gathered Rose

(1) Fold 1 short edge at a 90° angle.

(2) Fold bottom corner over at a 90° angle.

(3) Roll folded ribbon and secure. Gather-stitch half of remaining ribbon. Pull thread and wrap gather around folded ribbon.

(4) Gather-stitch remaining ribbon. Wrap gather around.

(5) Competed GATHERED ROSE.

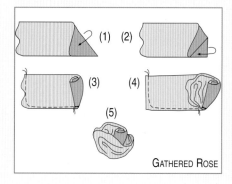

GATHERED ROSE

Grape

(1) Gather-stitch all 4 edges of a square of ribbon, ⅛" from edge.

(2) Pull thread to gather slightly.

(3) Place a small amount of stuffing in yo-yo.

(4) Pull thread tight to gather. Secure thread.

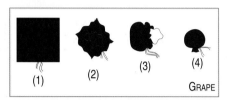

(1) (2) (3) (4)

GRAPE

Japanese Ribbon Stitch

(1) Come up through fabric at the starting point of stitch. Lay the ribbon flat on the fabric. At the end of the stitch, pierce the ribbon with the needle. Slowly pull the length of the ribbon through to the back, allowing the ends of the ribbon to curl. If the ribbon is pulled too tightly, the effect of the stitch can be lost. Vary the petals and leaves by adjusting the length, the tension of the ribbon before piercing, the position of piercing, and how loosely or tightly the ribbon is pulled down through itself.

(2) Completed JAPANESE RIBBON STITCH.

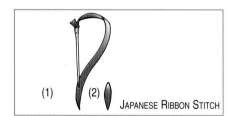

(1) (2)

JAPANESE RIBBON STITCH

Knife Pleats

Fold wired ribbon into ¼"-deep pleats, ½" apart, all in same direction. Stitch or glue in place on one long edge (See FLUTING diagram on page 15).

Knotted Lazy Daisy

(1) Make a LAZY DAISY loop.

(2) Wrap ribbon 2 times around needle. Insert needle into fabric at A. Push wraps down the needle to meet the fabric. Pull needle completely through fabric.

(3) Completed KNOTTED LAZY DAISY.

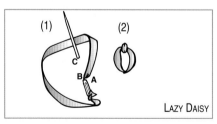

(1) (2) (3)

KNOTTED LAZY DAISY

Lazy Daisy

(1) Bring the needle up at A. Keep the ribbon flat, untwisted and full. Put the needle down through fabric at B and up at C, keeping the ribbon under the needle to form a loop. Pull the ribbon through, leaving the loop loose and full. To hold the loop in place, go down on other side of ribbon near C, forming a straight stitch over loop.

(2) Completed LAZY DAISY.

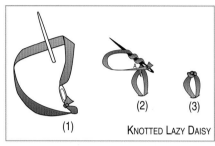

(1) (2)

LAZY DAISY

Marigold

Fold ribbon in half, matching selvages. Pin to hold. Trace 11 half circles onto ribbon so that straight edge of half circle is at ribbon fold.

Beginning at first half circle, secure thread, then gather-stitch around each half circle. Pull thread tightly to gather. Secure thread at end of

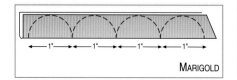

1"   1"   1"   1"

MARIGOLD

stitching. Shape petals so that all large petals are on one side of ribbon and all small petals are on other side of ribbon. Join last petal to first.

Fold top edge of small petals upwards, revealing orange edge of petals. Join all small orange petals in center.

Pansy

Note: Embellishing instructions will indicate dimensions for making specific PANSIES.

(1) Fold one long edge down. Pin to hold. Mark intervals.

(2) Fold on marks. Gather-stitch.

(3) Pull thread as tight as possible. Secure thread. Join petals together.

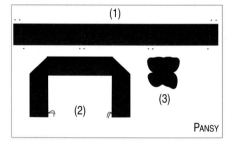

(1)

(2) (3)

PANSY

Pointed Petal Flower

(1) Press fabric in half, long edges together. Cut fabric into 15 lengths, each 3" long.

(2) Cut off edges as shown.

(3) Fold corners down, one to the front and one to the back.

(4) Repeat for 4 more petals. Stitch all 5 petals together for bottom layer of flower. Pull thread tightly to gather.

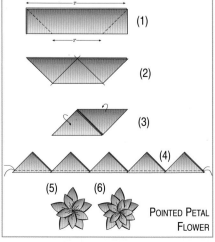

(1)

(2)

(3)

(4)

(5) (6)

POINTED PETAL FLOWER

(5) Fold and stitch another 5 pointed petals, placing stitching ⅛" higher than previous 5 pointed petals, creating smaller petals. Trim each petal ⅛" past stitching. Stitch these 5 petals together for middle layer of flower. Pull thread tightly to gather.

(6) Fold and stitch another 5 pointed petals, placing stitching ⅛" higher than previous 5 petals, and repeat. Stitch last 5 petals together for top layer of flower. Pull thread tightly to gather. Glue layers together, alternating petal placement.

Rosettes

For ⅛" rosette, cut 5" ribbon length; for ¼" rosette, cut 9" length. Mark center of ribbon length.

(1) Beginning at one end, fold end forward at right angle.

(2) Fold vertical ribbon forward at right angle. Continue folding ribbon forward at right angles. Roll to center mark. Secure, leaving needle and thread attached.

(3) Gather-stitch on edge of remaining ribbon length. Gather tightly. Wrap gathered ribbon around bud.

(4) Secure and fluff flower.

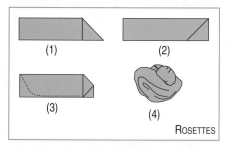

ROSETTES

Ruched Ribbon Flower

Note: Embellishing instructions will indicate the dimensions for making specific RUCHED RIBBON FLOWERS.

Starting at one end, lightly mark intervals with dull pencil along one edge. On remaining edge, lightly mark intervals, but offset the marks so that they occur halfway between the marks on the opposite edge. Using doubled thread in a matching color, gather-stitch in a zigzag pattern, connecting all the pencil marks. Pull thread to gently gather into cupped ruffles.

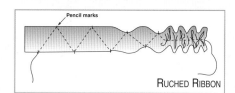

RUCHED RIBBON

Stem Stitch

Working from left to right, make slightly slanting stitches along the line of the stem. Come up at A, and insert needle through fabric at B. Bring needle up at C (halfway between A and B). Make all stitches the same length. Insert needle through fabric at D (half the length of the stitch beyond B). Bring needle up at the middle of previous stitch, and continue in the same manner.

STEM STITCH

Straight Stitch

This stitch may be taut or loose, depending on desired effect.

(1) Come up at A. Go down at B, keeping the ribbon flat.

(2) Completed Straight Stitch.

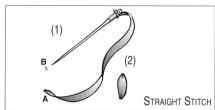

STRAIGHT STITCH

Squared Petal or Leaf

(1) The interval of the gathering stitches must be greater than the width of the ribbon to make a SQUARED PETAL or LEAF.

(2) Pull thread to gather and secure. Shape petal or leaf as desired (diagram on top of next column).

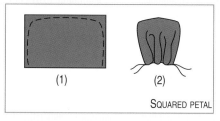

SQUARED PETAL

Turbans

(1) Fold fabric in half, matching short ends. Stitch ¼" seam.

(2) Finger-press seam open. Gather-stitch around one long edge.

(3) Pull thread tight to gather and secure thread.

(4) Stuff TURBAN.

(5) Turn under remaining raw edge ⅛", while gather stitching. Pull thread tight to gather and secure thread. Take thread down through center of turban to opposite side, then back up, and down again to tuft center.

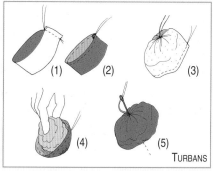

TURBANS

Twisted Japanese Ribbon Stitch

(1) Bring needle up at A. Extend ribbon its full length and twirl needle so ribbon coils but not so tight it buckles.

(2) Insert needle back into twisted ribbon at B.

(3) Pull needle through ribbon and fabric, allowing some of the ribbon to remain on the surface.

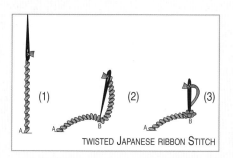

TWISTED JAPANESE RIBBON STITCH

SIMPLE   *Romantic*   ELEGANT

Chapter one

Classic

• *Cut Cardboard and Fabric*

• *Cover Cardboard with Fabric and Shape*

Laminate BOX SIDE with print outer fabric. Wrap sheer fabric over print fabric. Place wrong side up on work surface. Carefully roll with 1" dowel. Cover BASE and MIDDLE LID in same manner.

Pad LID with batting, then wrap with cotton print and sheer fabric.

Glue 3 INSIDE LIDS together. Laminate combined INSIDE LIDS with inside fabric. INSIDE BOTTOM is not wrapped with any fabric.

• *Assemble Box Bottom*

Follow instructions for *"Assembling Box Bottom"* of hinge-lid-style boxes on page 12. Slip INSIDE BOT-TOM 1/16" down from BOX SIDE'S edge. Remember that box does not have a ribbon hinge!

• *Line Box Bottom*

Follow instructions for *"Lining Strips"* of hinge-lid-style boxes on page 12. Glue INSIDE BOTTOM fabric onto LINING STRIP. Begin at center front of box and glue LINING STRIP to top edge of BOX SIDE.

• *Assemble Lid*

Center and glue wrong side of INSIDE LID to right side of MIDDLE LID. Flatten glue thoroughly.

• *Embellish and Finish Box*

Wrap 2"-wide white eyelet lace around box side. Wrap raw edge of lace to underside of box bottom. Overlap lace at center back.

Turn box upside down. Layer ⅜"-wide white organdy ribbon over ⅜"-wide lavender satin ribbon. Flute layered ribbons while gluing onto underside of box. Glue wrong side of BASE to bottom of box.

Wrap scraps of lace around left side of LID.

Embellish box following instructions below and diagram on page 22.

(A) Stitch 11 FOLDED PETALS with 1"-wide lavender sheer ribbon. Position petals on top of box and glue in place.

(B) Tie pale green and pale orchid 4mm ribbons into tiny bow. Glue bow in place, and cascade tails.

(C) Stitch brass hearts onto box top at right side.

(D) Cut pale iris 4mm ribbon into 5 lengths, each 5". Stitch each length into ROSETTE. Glue rosettes to top of brass hearts.

(E) Tie tiny bow with lt. iris and lt. orchid 7mm ribbons. Glue bow in place and drape tails.

(F) Glue buttons and beads to center of flower with industrial-strength adhesive. Stitch a few buttons and beads to cascaded ribbons.

Turn LID upside down. KNIFE-PLEAT ⅝"-wide green ombré wired ribbon into ¼"-deep pleats while gluing onto underside edge of LID. After pleating ribbon for 5 pleats, twist ribbon to bring opposite edge outward, and continue to pleat. Repeat, twisting after each 5 pleats until complete. Glue wrong side of LID to wrong side of MIDDLE LID.

Tools and Materials

Heavy cardboard–7" x 22"
Lightweight cardboard–4" x 16"
Outer fabrics (pansy print cotton and sheer dotted swiss)–17" x 12" each
Inside box fabric (pale green dotted moiré)–12" x 12"
Quilt batting–6" x 10"

24" of 2"-wide white eyelet lace
3" of scrap lace edging
1 yd. of ⅜"-wide lavender satin ribbon
1 yd. of ⅜"-wide white organdy ribbon
1 yd. of ⅝"-wide green ombré wired ribbon
1 yd. of 1"-wide lavender sheer ribbon; matching thread
25" of pale iris 4mm ribbon
22" each of pale green and pale orchid 4mm ribbon
12" each of lt. iris and lt. orchid 7mm ribbon
5 brass heart charms
10 assorted buttons and beads

Hand sewing needle
Size 3 crewel embroidery needle
Beading needle
Industrial-strength adhesive
1" wooden dowel

Heavy Cardboard	Light Cardboard	Inside Fabric	Outer Fabric
BASE and MIDDLE LID cut 2 LID INSIDE BOTTOM INSIDE LID-cut 3	LINING STRIP BOX SIDE	INSIDE LID + ¾"* INSIDE BOTTOM + 2¾"*	BASE and MIDDLE LID + ½"*-cut 2 LID + ¾"* BOX SIDE + ½"*

* See page 8.

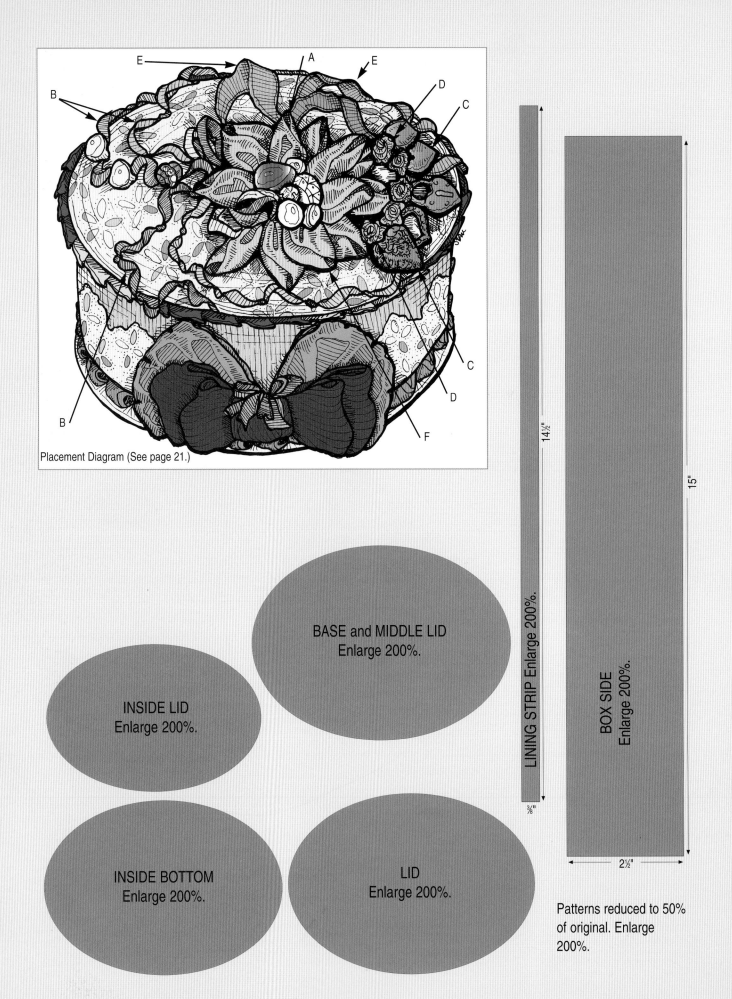

Placement Diagram (See page 21.)

LINING STRIP Enlarge 200%.

14½"

⅜"

BOX SIDE Enlarge 200%.

15"

2½"

BASE and MIDDLE LID
Enlarge 200%.

INSIDE LID
Enlarge 200%.

INSIDE BOTTOM
Enlarge 200%.

LID
Enlarge 200%.

Patterns reduced to 50%
of original. Enlarge
200%.

22

ROUND BOX

- *Cut Cardboard and Fabric*

- *Cover Cardboard with Fabric and Shape*

Laminate OUTSIDE BOX SIDE with outer fabric. Laminate INSIDE BOX SIDE with inside fabric.

Place OUTSIDE BOX SIDE wrong side up on work surface. Carefully roll with ½" dowel, beginning at outer short edge. Repeat process with INSIDE BOX SIDE, placing right side up on work surface.

Laminate BASE with outer fabric. Laminate INSIDE BOTTOM and INSIDE LID with inside fabric.

Follow instructions for *"Laminating Lid Strip"* of flask-style boxes on page 13. Laminate LID STRIP

Tools and Materials

Round Box

Heavy cardboard–6" x 6"
Lightweight cardboard–9" x 9"
Outer fabric (lt. green print cotton fabric)–4" x 12"
Inside box fabric (coordinating lt. green print cotton fabric)–8" x 15"
Quilt batting–3" square

9" of ⅝"-wide green ombré wired ribbon
18" of olive green braid

½" wooden dowel

Oval Box

Heavy cardboard–4" x 8"
Lightweight cardboard–8" x 9"
Outer fabric (flower print cotton)–6" x 12"
Inside box fabric (lt. pink bow print cotton)–5" x 15"
Quilt batting–3" square

18" of pale green 7mm textured ribbon
9" of ¼"-wide lt. green satin ribbon
3" of 1"-wide lt. green wired ribbon
12" of 1"-wide orange ombré wired ribbon; matching thread

Hand sewing needle
½" wooden dowel

with inside fabric. Place wrong side up on work surface. Carefully roll with ½" dowel, beginning at an outer edge.

Pad LID with batting, then wrap with inside fabric.

- *Assemble Box*

Follow instructions for *"Assembling Box Bottom"* of flask-style boxes on page 12.

- *Assemble Lid*

Follow instructions for *"Assembling Lid"* of flask-style boxes on page 13. Turn padded LID upside down. Glue edge of olive green braid to underside edge of lid. Glue LID to top of assembled lid.

- *Embellish Box*

Trim bottom edge of box with ⅝"-wide green ombré wired ribbon. Add olive green braid over ribbon.

OVAL BOX

- *Cut Cardboard and Fabric*

- *Cover Cardboard with Fabric and Shape*

Laminate OUTSIDE BOX SIDE with outer fabric. Laminate INSIDE BOX SIDE with inside fabric.

Place OUTSIDE BOX SIDE on work surface, wrong side up. Carefully roll with ½" dowel, beginning at outer short edge. Repeat process with INSIDE BOX SIDE, placing on work surface right side up.

Laminate BASE with outer fabric. Laminate INSIDE BOTTOM and INSIDE LID with inside fabric.

Follow instructions for *"Laminating Lid Strip"* of flask-style boxes on page 13. Laminate LID STRIP with outer fabric. Place on work surface, wrong side up. Carefully roll with ½" dowel, beginning at an outer edge.

Pad LID with batting, then wrap with inside fabric.

- *Assemble Box*

Follow instructions for *"Assembling Box Bottom"* of flask-style boxes on page 12.

- *Assemble Lid*

Follow instructions for *"Assembling Lid"* of flask-style boxes on page 13. Turn padded LID upside down. FLUTE pale green 7mm textured ribbon while gluing to underside edge of LID. Glue LID to top of assembled lid.

- *Embellish Box*

Trim bottom edge of box with ¼"-wide lt. green satin ribbon. Stitch a FOLDED LEAF with 1"-wide green wired ribbon.

Stitch a GATHERED ROSE, using 9" of 1"-wide orange ombré wired ribbon, but do not cut remaining ribbon. Gather-stitch to opposite ribbon edge and stitch 2 SQUARED PETALS. Pull gathers and secure to flower. Glue leaf and flower to box top.

Heavy Cardboard	Light Cardboard
All Four Boxes	**All Four Boxes**
BASE	INSIDE BOX SIDE
LID and INSIDE LID–cut 2	OUTSIDE BOX SIDE
INSIDE BOTTOM	LID STRIP

HEART BOX

• *Cut Cardboard and Fabric, Score*

• *Cover Cardboard with Fabric and Shape*

Laminate OUTSIDE BOX SIDE with outer fabric. Laminate INSIDE BOX SIDE with inside fabric.

Place OUTSIDE BOX SIDE on work surface, wrong side up. Fold at score mark and emphasize score. Carefully roll with ½" dowel, beginning at each outer edge and rolling toward center score. Repeat process with INSIDE BOX SIDE, placing on work surface right side up.

Laminate BASE with outer fabric. Laminate INSIDE BOTTOM and INSIDE LID with inside fabric.

Follow instructions for *"Laminating Lid Strip"* of flask-style boxes on page 13. Laminate unscored side of LID STRIP with outer fabric.

Scored side of cardboard is the outside of LID STRIP. Place unscored side up on work surface. Fold in half at score mark and emphasize score. Carefully roll unscored side up with ½" dowel, beginning at each outer edge and rolling toward score.

Pad LID with batting, then wrap with inside fabric.

• *Assemble Box*

Follow instructions for *"Assembling Box Bottom"* of flask-style boxes on page 12.

• *Assemble Lid*

Follow instructions for *"Assembling Lid"* of flask-style boxes on page 13.

Glue LID to top of assembled lid.

• *Embellish Box*

Trim bottom edge of box with beige 9mm textured ribbon. Trim bottom edge and lid edge with tiny pink picot trim. Stitch ROSETTE with 9" of beige 9mm textured ribbon. Glue to center top edge of box. Tie tiny bow with pale pink and rose 4mm silk ribbons. Glue and drape. Tie a tiny bow with remaining beige ribbon. Glue to center back at base of box.

PRISM BOX

• *Cut Cardboard and Fabric, Score*

• *Cover Cardboard with Fabric and Shape*

Laminate scored side of OUTSIDE BOX SIDE with outer fabric. Laminate unscored side of INSIDE BOX SIDE with inside fabric.

Place OUTSIDE BOX SIDE wrong side up on work surface. Fold at each score mark and emphasize score. Repeat process with INSIDE BOX SIDE, placing right side up on work surface.

Laminate BASE with outer fabric. Laminate INSIDE BOTTOM and INSIDE LID with inside fabric.

Follow instructions for *"Laminating Lid Strip"* of flask-style boxes on page 13. Cover unscored side of LID STRIP with inside fabric. Place glued LID STRIP ¼" up from 1 long edge of fabric and centered between short edges and trim. Scored side of cardboard is the outside of LID STRIP. Place on work surface, unscored side up. Fold at each score mark and emphasize score.

Pad LID with batting, then wrap with inside fabric.

• *Assemble Box*

Follow instructions for *"Assembling Box Bottom"* of flask-style

* See page 8.

Heavy Cardboard	*Light Cardboard*	*Inside Fabric*	*Outer Fabric*
Inside Fabric	**Inside Fabric**	**Inside Fabric**	**Inside Fabric**
INSIDE BOX SIDE + ¾"*	INSIDE BOX SIDE + ¾"*	INSIDE BOX SIDE + ¾"*	INSIDE BOX SIDE + ¾"*
INSIDE LID + ½"*	INSIDE LID + ½"*	INSIDE LID + ½"*	INSIDE LID + ½"*
INSIDE BOTTOM + ½"*	INSIDE BOTTOM + ½"*	INSIDE BOTTOM + ½"*	INSIDE BOTTOM + ½"*
LID + ¾"*			LID + ¾"*
LID STRIP-2¼" x 8¾"			LID STRIP-2¼" x 8¼"
Outside Fabric	**Outside Fabric**	**Outside Fabric**	**Outside Fabric**
OUTSIDE BOX SIDE + ½"*	OUTSIDE BOX SIDE + ½"*	OUTSIDE BOX SIDE + ½"*	OUTSIDE BOX SIDE + ½"*
BASE + ½"*	BASE + ½"*	BASE + ½"*	BASE + ½"*
	LID + ¾"*	LID + ¾"*	
	LID STRIP-2¼" x 9"	LID STRIP-2¼" x 8"	

Tools and Materials

Heart Box
Heavy cardboard–6" x 6"
Lightweight cardboard–6" x 8"
Outer fabric (small pink flower print cotton)–6" x 12"
Inside box fabric (large pink flower print cotton)–4" x 15"
Quilt batting–3" square

27" of beige 9mm textured ribbon; matching thread
14" of tiny pink picot trim
12" each of pale pink and rose 4mm silk ribbon

Hand sewing needle
1" and ½" wooden dowel

Prism Box
Heavy cardboard–6" x 6"
Lightweight cardboard–10" x 10"
Outer fabric (large rose print black cotton)–12" x 5"
Inside box fabric (small flower print black cotton)–8" x 12"
Quilt batting–3" square

18" of ¼"-wide burgundy velvet ribbon
18" of 1"-wide burgundy sheer picot-edged ribbon

1" wooden dowel

boxes on page 12. Begin gluing at any corner and rotating OUTSIDE BOX SIDE. Join 1 side.

• *Assemble Lid*

Follow instructions for *"Assembling Lid"* of flask-style boxes on page 13.

Turn padded LID upside down. Flute ¼"-wide burgundy velvet ribbon while gluing to underside edge of LID. Glue LID to top of assembled lid.

• *Embellish Box*

Trim bottom edge of box with 1"-wide burgundy sheer picot-edged ribbon. With remaining ribbon, stitch a 2"-wide flat bow. Glue flat bow over ribbon joint.

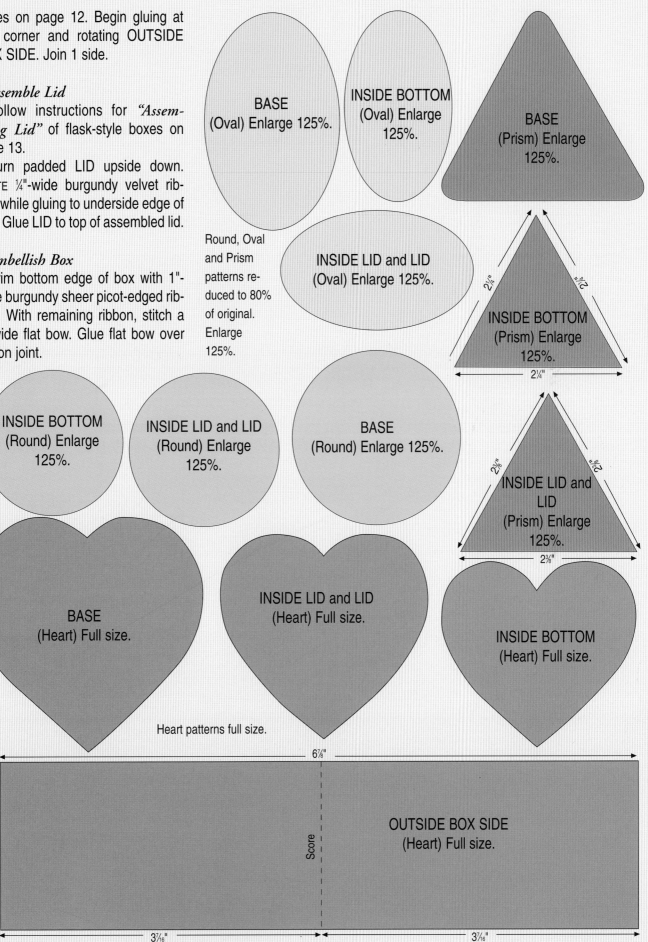

BASE
(Oval) Enlarge 125%.

INSIDE BOTTOM
(Oval) Enlarge 125%.

BASE
(Prism) Enlarge 125%.

Round, Oval and Prism patterns reduced to 80% of original. Enlarge 125%.

INSIDE LID and LID
(Oval) Enlarge 125%.

INSIDE BOTTOM
(Prism) Enlarge 125%.

2¼"
2⅜"
2¼"

INSIDE BOTTOM
(Round) Enlarge 125%.

INSIDE LID and LID
(Round) Enlarge 125%.

BASE
(Round) Enlarge 125%.

INSIDE LID and LID
(Prism) Enlarge 125%.

2⅜"
2⅜"
2⅜"

BASE
(Heart) Full size.

INSIDE LID and LID
(Heart) Full size.

INSIDE BOTTOM
(Heart) Full size.

Heart patterns full size.

6⅞"

Score

OUTSIDE BOX SIDE
(Heart) Full size.

1¾"

3⁷⁄₁₆"

3⁷⁄₁₆"

27

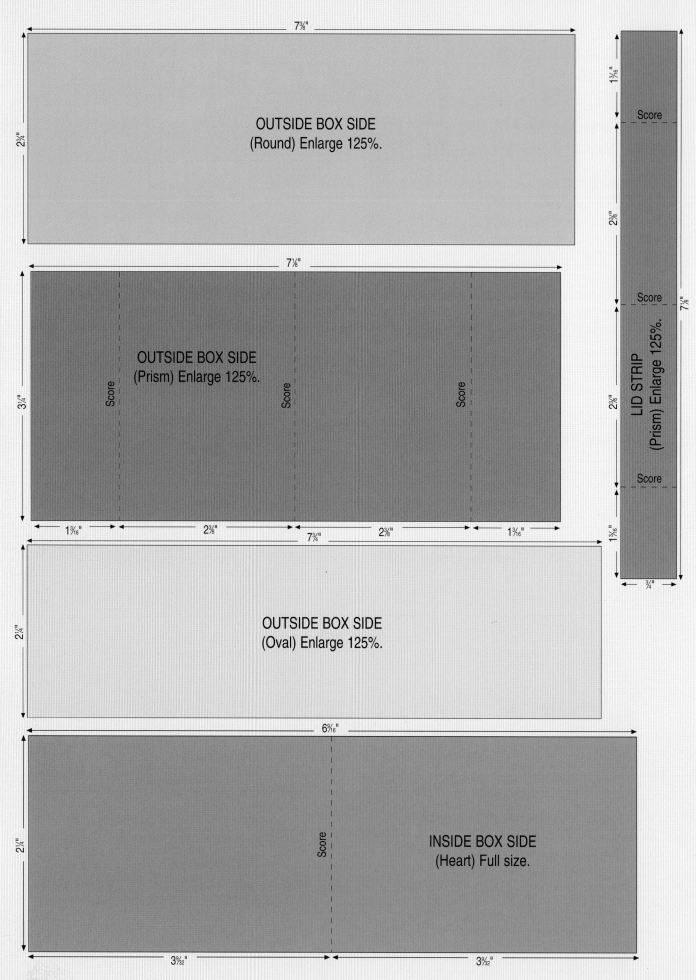

OUTSIDE BOX SIDE
(Round) Enlarge 125%.

7⅞"

2¾"

OUTSIDE BOX SIDE
(Prism) Enlarge 125%.

7⅛"

3¾"

Score

Score

Score

1³⁄₁₆"   2⅜"   2⅜"   1³⁄₁₆"

7¾"

OUTSIDE BOX SIDE
(Oval) Enlarge 125%.

2¼"

LID STRIP
(Prism) Enlarge 125%.

Score

Score

Score

Score

1³⁄₁₆"

2⅜"

2⅜"

2⅜"

1³⁄₁₆"

7⅞"

¾"

INSIDE BOX SIDE
(Heart) Full size.

6⁹⁄₁₆"

2¼"

Score

3⁹⁄₃₂"   3⁹⁄₃₂"

28

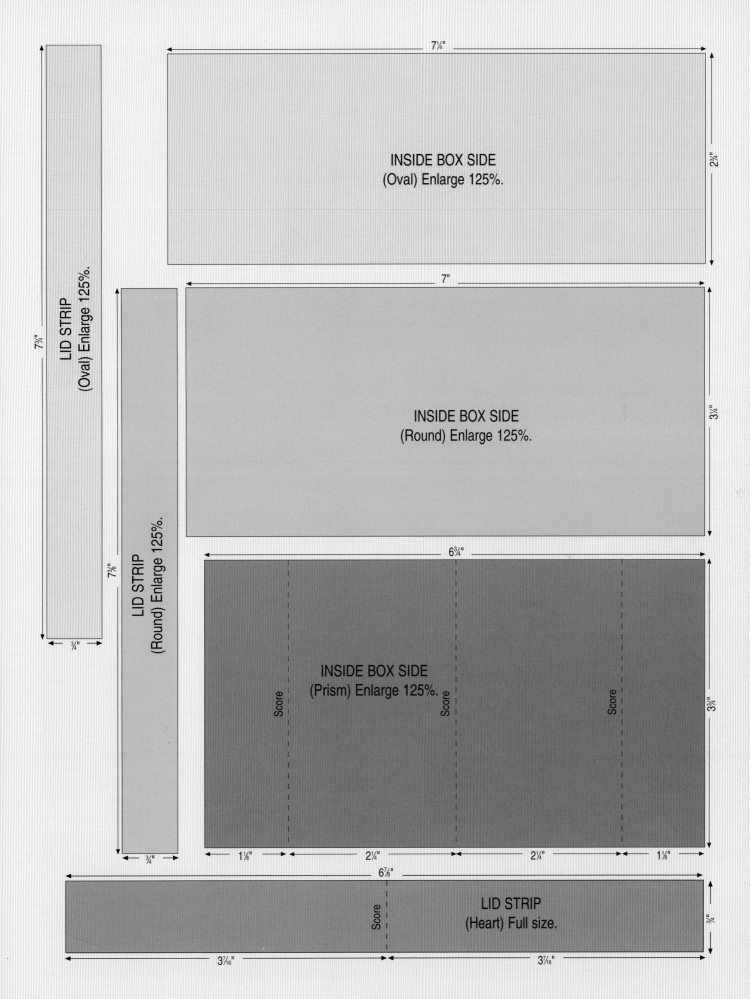

INSIDE BOX SIDE
(Oval) Enlarge 125%.

7¼"

2¾"

LID STRIP
(Oval) Enlarge 125%.

7¾"

¾"

INSIDE BOX SIDE
(Round) Enlarge 125%.

7"

3¼"

LID STRIP
(Round) Enlarge 125%.

7⅞"

¾"

INSIDE BOX SIDE
(Prism) Enlarge 125%.

6¾"

3¾"

Score

Score

Score

1⅛"

2¼"

2¼"

1⅛"

LID STRIP
(Heart) Full size.

6⅞"

¾"

Score

3⁷⁄₁₆"

3⁷⁄₁₆"

• Cut Cardboard and Fabric

• Cover Cardboard with Fabric

Wrap BOX SIDE, BASE and MIDDLE LID with outer fabric. Pad INSIDE LID with batting, then wrap with inside fabric. INSIDE BOTTOM is not wrapped with any fabric. Embellish LID before pad and wrap process.

• Assemble Box Bottom

Follow instructions for *"Assembling Box Bottom"* of hinge-lid-style boxes on page 12. Cut 2 pieces of ⅝"-wide aqua variegated ribbon, each 2" long. Glue each piece of ribbon to inside top edge of box, ½" from center back for each.

Wrap ⅞"-wide mauve jacquard ribbon around lower edge of box. Cover unfinished edge with half of doubled, flat bow from same ribbon.

FLUTE 1¼ yd. of ½"-wide plum ribbon while gluing onto underside of box.

Cut 6 pieces from ⅞"-wide mauve jacquard ribbon, each 3½" long.

Gather-stitch 1 long edge of each ribbon length. Pull thread as tight as possible and secure thread. Place box bottom on BASE. Mark position of hexagon points. Glue gathered, raw edge of ribbon to underside edge of box bottom at each point of hexagon. Glue BASE to box bottom.

• Line Box Bottom

Follow instructions for *"Lining Strips"* of hinge-lid-style boxes on page 12. Glue INSIDE BOTTOM fabric onto LINING STRIP. Glue LINING STRIP around top inside edge of BOX SIDE.

• Glue Ribbon Hinge to Inside Lid

Follow instructions for *"Gluing Ribbon Hinge to Inside Lid"* on page 12.

• Embellish and Finish Box

Embellish box following instructions below and diagram on page 32.

(A) Cut ¾"-wide plum ombré ribbon into 11 lengths, each ¾" long. Stitch each as a GRAPE.

(B) Fold 9" of ½"-wide plum ribbon into 5 FOLDED PETALS. Gather-stitch petals together in a chain. Secure thread.

(C) Cut a 7" length from ⅞"-wide mauve jacquard ribbon and stuff as for a TURBAN.

(D) Stitch 2 SQUARED LEAVES with ⅝"-wide purple and green iridescent ribbon, 3½" for each leaf.

(E) Tie a tiny bow with thistle and grey green 4mm ribbons and glue in place. CASCADE ribbon tails.

Stitch embellishments to LID fabric, using a beading needle.

Sew a bead into center of each grape and turban. Pad and wrap embellished fabric to LID.

(F) Glue brass charm in place with industrial-strength adhesive.

Glue embellished LID to MIDDLE LID. Glue narrow magenta cording between LID and MIDDLE LID.

Tools and Materials
Heavy cardboard-10" x 17"
Lightweight cardboard-15" x 3½"
Outer fabric (dusty aqua silk jacquard)- 16" x 10"
Inside box fabric (deep magenta jacquard)-12" x 15"
Quilt batting-6" x 12"
2 yds. of ⅞"-wide mauve jacquard ribbon
½ yd. of narrow magenta cording
1½ yd. of ½"-wide plum ribbon
1½ yd. of ¾"-wide plum ombré ribbon
⅝ yd. each of thistle and grey green 4mm ribbon
7" of ⅝"-wide purple and green iridescent ribbon
Brass charm
Seed beads
Hand sewing needle
Beading needle
Industrial-strength adhesive

Heavy Cardboard	Light Cardboard	Inside Fabric	Outer Fabric
INSIDE LID INSIDE BOTTOM LID BASE and MIDDLE LID- cut 2	LINING STRIP BOX SIDE	INSIDE BOTTOM + **3**"* INSIDE LID + ¾"*	BASE and MIDDLE LID + ½"*-cut 2 LID + ¾"* BOX SIDE + ½"*

* See page 8.

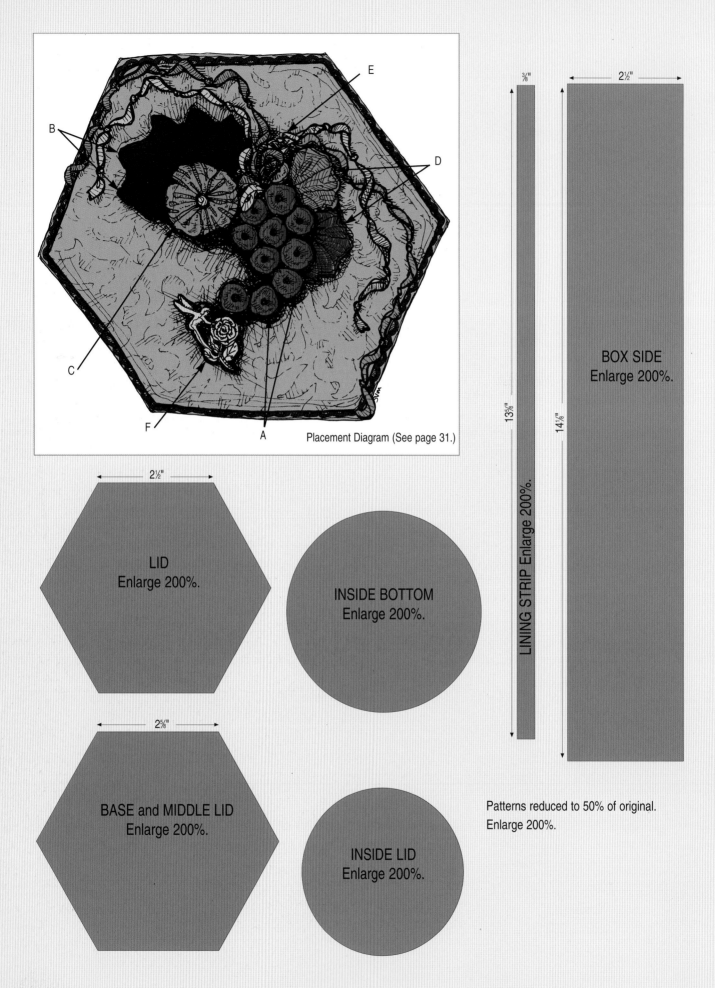

E

B

D

C

F   A   Placement Diagram (See page 31.)

⅜"

2½"

BOX SIDE
Enlarge 200%.

13⅝"

14⅛"

LINING STRIP Enlarge 200%.

2½"

LID
Enlarge 200%.

INSIDE BOTTOM
Enlarge 200%.

2⅝"

BASE and MIDDLE LID
Enlarge 200%.

INSIDE LID
Enlarge 200%.

Patterns reduced to 50% of original.
Enlarge 200%.

LARGE HEART BOX

• *Cut Cardboard and Fabric, Score*

• *Cover Cardboard with Fabric*

Laminate scored side of BOX SIDE with outer fabric, then wrap gold lace around BOX SIDE. Fold in half, wrong sides together, and emphasize score. Carefully roll with 1" dowel, beginning at each outer edge and rolling toward center score.

Laminate BASE and MIDDLE LID with jacquard, then wrap with gold lace. Pad LID with batting, then wrap with jacquard. Repeat with gold lace. Pad INSIDE LID with batting, then

wrap with inside fabric. INSIDE BOTTOM is not wrapped with fabric.

• *Assemble Box Bottom*

Follow instructions for *"Assembling Box Bottom"* of hinge-lid-style boxes on page 12. Cut 2 pieces of gold 7mm silk ribbon, each 2½" long. Glue each piece of ribbon to inside top edge of box, 1" from each side of center back.

• *Line Box Bottom*

Follow instructions for *"Lining Strips"* of hinge-lid-style boxes on page 12. Glue INSIDE BOTTOM fabric onto LINING STRIP. Begin gluing LINING STRIP at tip of heart to top edge of BOX SIDE.

• *Glue Ribbon Hinge to Inside Lid*

Follow instructions for *"Gluing Ribbon Hinge to Inside Lid"* on page 12.

• *Embellish and Finish Box*

Glue narrow gold soutache braid to bottom edge of box. Turn box upside down. FLUTE gold 7mm silk ribbon while gluing onto underside of box. Glue wrong side of BASE to underside of box bottom. Wrap scrap of pale yellow lace to top of LID.

Embellish box following instructions below and diagram on page 37.

(A) Stitch 10 ROSETTES with 4mm silk ribbon, using one 5"-length each.

(B) Stitch 2 GATHERED ROSES, layering 9" of 7mm brown organdy ribbon over 9" of beige and rose 7mm silk ribbon.

(C) Stitch 2 RUCHED RIBBON FLOWERS from both ⅝"-wide gold and rose wired ribbon. Intervals are ¾" apart. Arrange all flowers, then glue in place.

(D) Tie a tiny bow with beige and pink 4mm ribbon, 18" each shade. Glue bow in place. Cascade tails, using crewel embroidery needle.

(E) Stitch 2 BULLION ROSES with gold and rose silk floss.

Use beading needle to stitch each button in place. Drape tiny ivory picot trim, and glue in place.

Glue embellished LID to MIDDLE LID. Glue brass charms in place with industrial-strength adhesive. Glue narrow antique gold metallic cord between LID and MIDDLE LID.

SMALL HEART BOX

• *Cut Cardboard and Fabric, Score*

• *Cover Cardboard with Fabric*

Wrap scored side of BOX SIDE with outer fabric. Fold in half, wrong sides together, and emphasize score. Carefully roll with ½" dowel, beginning at each outer edge and rolling toward center score.

Wrap BASE and MIDDLE LID with outer fabric. Pad INSIDE LID with batting, then wrap with inside fabric.

Tools and Materials

Large Heart Box
Heavy cardboard–16" x 11"
Lightweight cardboard–4" x 15"
Outer fabric (pale gold jacquard and gold lace)–12" x 22"
Inside box fabric (pink and gold satin)–10" x 15"
Quilt batting–5" x 10"

Scrap of pale yellow lace
9" of tiny ivory picot trim
15" of narrow antique gold metallic cord
15" of narrow gold soutache braid
1 yard gold 7mm silk ribbon
Gold and rose silk floss
5" each of dk., med., and lt. rose; dk., med., and lt. beige; grey, mauve, coral and olive green 4mm silk ribbon
18" each of beige and pink 4mm silk ribbon
9" each of beige and rose 7mm silk ribbon; matching thread
18" of brown 7mm organdy ribbon
11" of ⅝"-wide gold and rose wired ribbon; matching thread
5 tiny brown mother-of-pearl buttons
1 mother-of-pearl fan button
Brass charms–watering can and angel

Size 3 crewel embroidery needle
Hand sewing needle

Heavy Cardboard	Light Cardboard	Inside Fabric	Outer Fabric
Both Boxes INSIDE LID INSIDE BOTTOM BASE and MIDDLE LID- cut 2 LID	**Both Boxes** BOX SIDE LINING STRIP	**Small Heart Box** Inside BOTTOM + 1¾"* INSIDE LID + ½"* **Large Heart Box** INSIDE BOTTOM + 2¾"* INSIDE LID + ½"*	**Both Boxes** BOX SIDE, BASE and MIDDLE LID + ½"* LID + ¾"*

* See page 8.

INSIDE BOTTOM is not wrapped with any fabric. Embroider LID before pad and wrap process.

• Assemble Box Bottom

Follow instructions for *"Assembling Box Bottom"* of hinge-lid-style boxes on page 12. Cut 2 pieces of ¼"-wide beige satin ribbon, each 2" long. Glue each piece of ribbon to inside top edge of box, ½" from center back for each.

• Line Box Bottom

Follow instructions for *"Lining Strips"* of hinge-lid-style boxes on page 12. Glue INSIDE BOTTOM fabric onto LINING STRIP. Begin gluing LINING STRIP at tip of heart to top edge of BOX SIDE.

• Glue Ribbon Hinge to Inside Lid

Follow instructions for *"Gluing Ribbon Hinge to Inside Lid"* on page 12.

• Embellish and Finish Box

Glue 1"-wide ivory lace around bottom side edge of box. Turn box upside down. FLUTE ¼"-wide beige satin ribbon while gluing onto underside of box. Glue wrong side of BASE to underside of bottom of box. Wrap a bit of lace along top right edge of LID.

Following stitch guide and chart below, embroider LID.

Pad LID with batting, then wrap with outer fabric. Glue wrong side of LID to wrong side of MIDDLE LID. Flatten glue. Glue 2 rows of ivory narrow cording to edge of LID. Tie a tiny bow with ivory and lt. beige silk floss and glue to inside of box at center back.

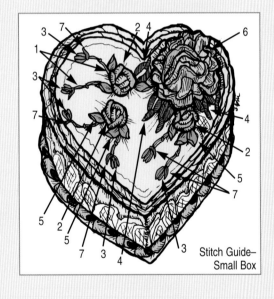

Stitch Guide– Small Box

#	Stitch	Ribbon or Floss
1	COUCHING	3 strands of olive green floss
2	BULLION ROSES	Pale pink and lt. beige silk floss
3	STRAIGHT STITCH	6 strands rose floss
4	BULLION LAZY DAISY	Dk. olive green floss
5	RIBBON STITCH	Grey-green 4mm silk ribbon
6	GATHERED ROSE	Pink silk and ivory textured 7mm ribbon
7	STRAIGHT STITCH	Dk. olive green floss

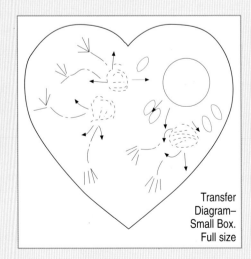

Transfer Diagram– Small Box. Full size

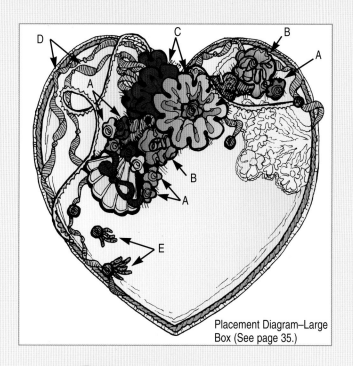

Placement Diagram–Large
Box (See page 35.)

Patterns for Small Heart Box full size. Patterns for Large Heart Box reduced to 50% of original. Enlarge 200%.

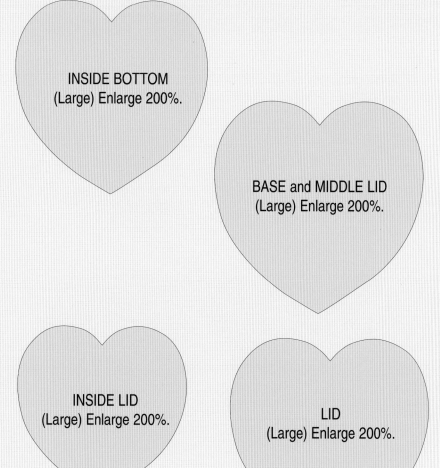

INSIDE BOTTOM
(Large) Enlarge 200%.

BASE and MIDDLE LID
(Large) Enlarge 200%.

INSIDE LID
(Large) Enlarge 200%.

LID
(Large) Enlarge 200%.

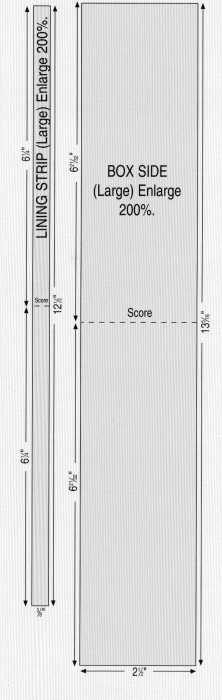

LINING STRIP (Large) Enlarge 200%.

BOX SIDE
(Large) Enlarge
200%.

Score

Score

6¼"

6²¹/₃₂"

12½"

13⁵/₁₆"

6¼"

6²¹/₃₂"

³/₈"

2½"

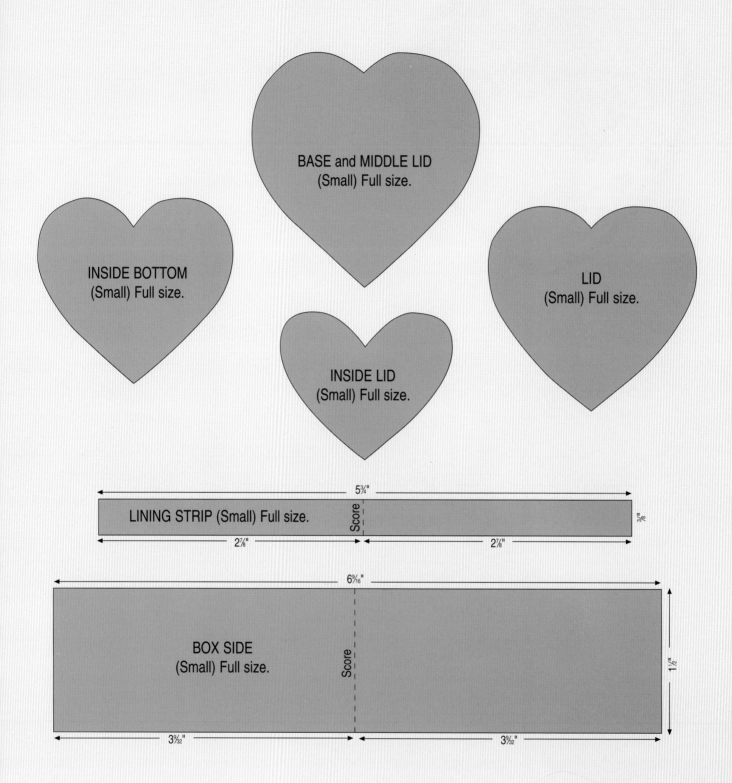

BASE and MIDDLE LID
(Small) Full size.

INSIDE BOTTOM
(Small) Full size.

LID
(Small) Full size.

INSIDE LID
(Small) Full size.

LINING STRIP (Small) Full size.
Score
5¾"
2⅞"
2⅞"
⅜"

BOX SIDE
(Small) Full size.
Score
6⁹⁄₁₆"
3⁹⁄₃₂"
3⁹⁄₃₂"
1½"

Feminine *Delicate* SPLENDID

Chapter two

Exquisite

Diamonds Are Forever

• Cut Cardboard and Fabric, Score

• Cover Cardboard with Fabric

Wrap scored side of BOX SIDE with outer fabric. Fold at each score mark, and emphasize scores.

Wrap BASE and MIDDLE LID with outer fabric. Pad LID with batting, then wrap with outer fabric. Glue three layers of INSIDE LID together. Pad combined INSIDE LID with batting, then wrap with inside fabric. INSIDE BOTTOM is not wrapped with fabric.

• Assemble Box Bottom

Follow instructions for *"Assembling Box Bottom"* of hinge-lid-style boxes on page 12. Slip INSIDE BOTTOM into BOX SIDE 1/16" from bottom.

• Line Box Bottom

Follow instructions for *"Lining Strips"* of hinge-lid-style boxes on page 12. Glue INSIDE BOTTOM fabric onto LINING STRIP. Begin gluing at tip of diamond. Remember this box does not have a ribbon hinge!

• Assemble Lid

Center and glue wrong side of INSIDE LIDS to right side of MIDDLE LID. Flatten glue thoroughly.

• Embellish and Finish Box

Glue 1/4"-wide off-white French Val lace to side edge of box, 3/16" up from bottom edge. Glue 1/4"-wide ivory velvet ribbon to bottom side edge of box.

Turn box upside down. Cut 16" from French Val lace. Gather to fit, and glue edge of lace to underside edge of bottom of box. Glue wrong side of BASE to bottom of box.

Wrap bits of lace and velvet ribbon around top right edge of LID.

Embellish box following instructions and diagram below.

(A) Stitch a ROSETTE with ivory 7mm textured ribbon.

(B) Stitch a GATHERED ROSE with 1/4"-wide off-white French Val lace. Glue both roses in place.

(C) Sew buttons and beads onto box top using beading needle.

Turn LID upside down. Glue edge of off-white French Val lace to underside edge of LID. Give lace extra ease at points so it will remain flat.

Glue wrong side of LID to wrong side of MIDDLE LID.

(D) Tie tiny bow with gold metallic narrow ribbon. Glue in place and drape tails.

Tools and Materials

Heavy cardboard–5" x 10"
Lightweight cardboard–3" x 8"
Outer fabric (ivory silk)–9" x 8"
Inside box fabric (blue tie-dyed silk)–
  9" x 8"
Quilt batting–3" x 5"

1½" yd. of 1/4"-wide off-white French Val
  lace; matching thread
12" of 1/4"-wide ivory velvet ribbon
9" of ivory textured 7mm ribbon, matching thread
7" of gold metallic narrow ribbon
7 mother of pearl buttons
2 crystal beads
Several pearl beads

Hand sewing needle
Beading needle
1" wooden dowel

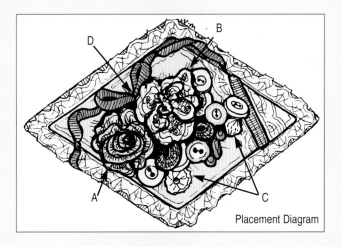

Placement Diagram

Heavy Cardboard	Light Cardboard	Inside Fabric	Outer Fabric
BASE and MIDDLE LID-cut 2 LID INSIDE BOTTOM INSIDE LID-cut 3	LINING STRIP BOX SIDE	INSIDE LID + 3/4"* INSIDE BOTTOM + 2½"*	BASE and MIDDLE LID + ½"*-cut 2 LID + 3/4"* BOX SIDE + ½"*

* See page 8.

Patterns full size.

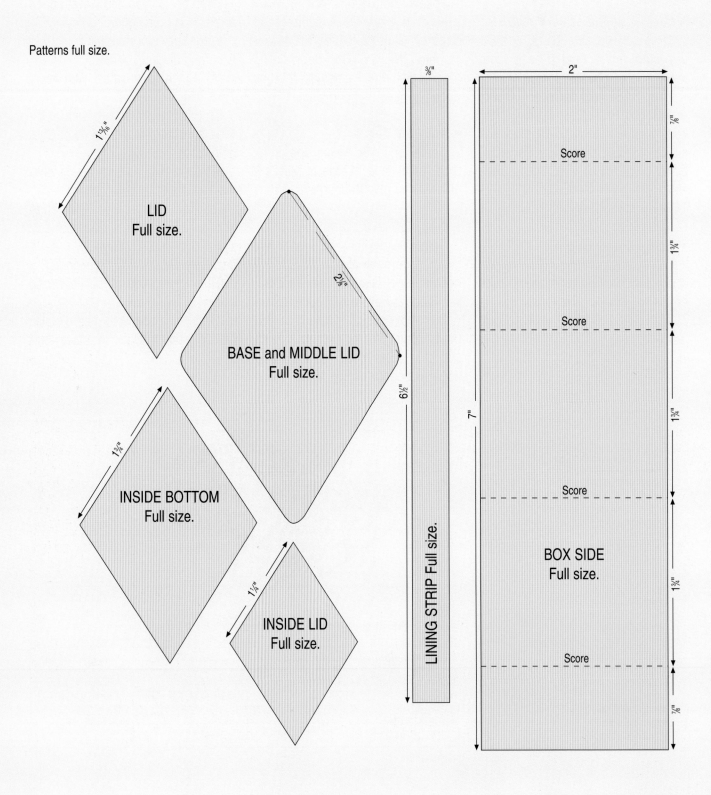

LID
Full size.

1 13/16 "

BASE and MIDDLE LID
Full size.

2 1/8 "

INSIDE BOTTOM
Full size.

1 3/4 "

INSIDE LID
Full size.

1 1/2 "

3/8"

6 1/2"

LINING STRIP Full size.

2"

7"

Score

7/8"

1 3/4"

Score

1 3/4"

Score

BOX SIDE
Full size.

1 3/4"

Score

7/8"

44

• *Cut Cardboard and Fabric, Score*

• *Cover Cardboard with Fabric and Shape*

Laminate scored side of OUTSIDE BOX SIDE with outer fabric. Laminate unscored side of INSIDE BOX SIDE with inside fabric.

Place OUTSIDE BOX SIDE wrong side up on work surface. Fold at each score mark and emphasize scores. Place INSIDE BOX SIDE right side up on work surface. Fold at each score mark and emphasize scores.

Laminate BASE with outer fabric. Laminate INSIDE BOTTOM and INSIDE LID with inside fabric.

Scored side of cardboard is the outside of LID STRIP. Follow instructions for *"Laminating Lid Strip"* of flask-style boxes on page 13. Cover unscored side of LID STRIP with in-side fabric. Place narrowest long edge of glued LID STRIP ¼" up from 1 long edge of fabric and centered between short edges. Top edge of fabric will ruffle slightly because fabric strip does not match LID STRIP exactly. Place unscored side up on work surface. Fold at each score mark and emphasize scores.

Pad LID with batting, then wrap with inside fabric.

• *Assemble Box*

Follow instructions for *"Assembling Box Bottom"* of flask-style boxes on page 12. Slip INSIDE BOTTOM into box side, ⅟₁₆" down from INSIDE BOX SIDE'S largest end. Begin gluing in place at any corner with a thin bead of hot glue.

Gather French Val lace and glue edge of lace to underside edge of box bottom. Glue wrong side of BASE to bottom of box.

• *Assemble Lid*

Follow instructions for *"Assembling Lid"* of flask-style boxes on page 12. Wrap LID STRIP around INSIDE LID at narrowest edge. Slip INSIDE LID into LID STRIP edge with extended fabric at narrowest edge.

• *Embellish and Finish Box*

Cut country blue 7mm ribbon in half. Turn padded LID upside down. Center and glue edge of each ribbon half to underside short edge of LID. Glue right side of padded LID to assembled lid, keeping ribbons extended.

Glue tiny picot trim to box top lid. Tie ribbons in bow, knot tails.

Tools and Materials
Heavy cardboard–6" x 6"
Lightweight cardboard–8" x 12"
Outer fabric (large rose print cotton)–4" x 15"
Inside box fabric (light blue geometric print cotton)–7" x 15"
Quilt batting–2" square
18" of narrow French Val lace
18" of country blue 7mm ribbon
8" of tiny picot trim
1" wooden dowel

Heavy Cardboard	Light Cardboard	Inside Fabric	Outer Fabric
BASE	INSIDE BOX SIDE	INSIDE BOX SIDE + ¾"*	OUTSIDE BOX SIDE + ½"*
LID and INSIDE LID -cut 2	OUTSIDE BOX SIDE	LID + ¾"*	BASE + ½"*
INSIDE BOTTOM	LID STRIP	INSIDE LID + ½"*	
		INSIDE BOTTOM + ½"*	
		LID STRIP 2¼" x 9¼"	

* See page 8.

Patterns reduced to 80% of original. Enlarge 125%.

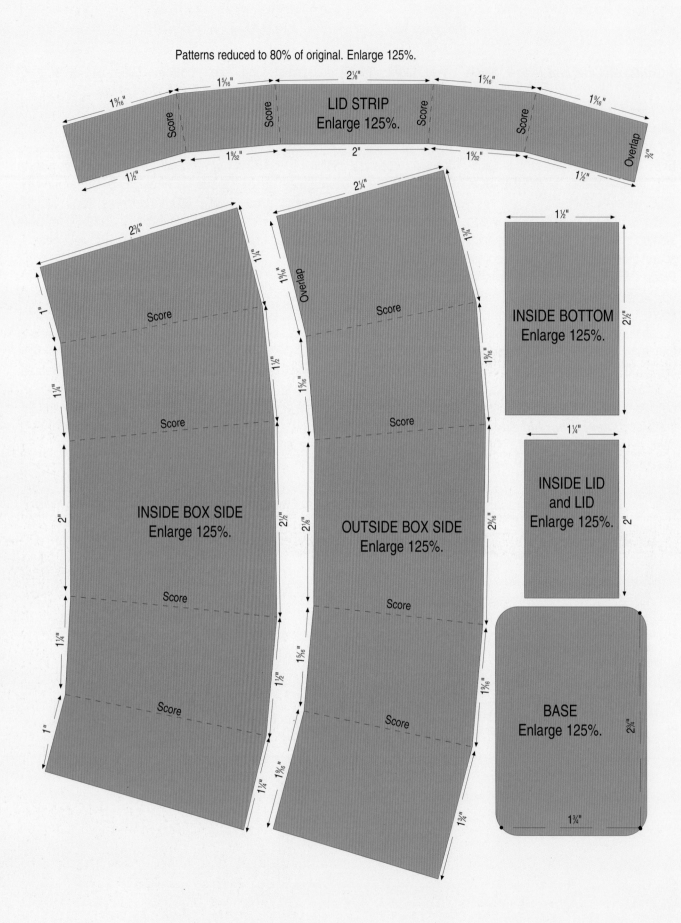

LID STRIP
Enlarge 125%.

INSIDE BOX SIDE
Enlarge 125%.

OUTSIDE BOX SIDE
Enlarge 125%.

INSIDE BOTTOM
Enlarge 125%.

INSIDE LID
and LID
Enlarge 125%.

BASE
Enlarge 125%.

Score

Overlap

• *Cut Cardboard and Fabric, Score*

• *Cover Cardboard with Fabric and Shape*

Laminate unscored side of BOX SIDE with outer fabric. Place right side up on work surface. Fold at each score mark and emphasize score.

Place BOX SIDE wrong side up on work surface. Carefully roll with 1" dowel, beginning at an outer edge, and roll toward a score. Use ½" dowel to add extra shape to centers of each section. Stand BOX SIDE up. Pinch at each score mark.

Laminate BASE and MIDDLE LID with outer fabric. Pad INSIDE LID with 1 layer of batting, then wrap with inside fabric. INSIDE BOTTOM is not wrapped with fabric. Embroider LID before pad and wrap process.

• *Assemble Box Bottom*

Follow instructions for *"Assembling Box Bottom"* of hinge-lid-style boxes on page 12. Slip INSIDE BOTTOM into BOX SIDE 1/16" down from edge. Begin gluing in place at any

score line. Match each score line with dip of each flower scallop. Emphasize flower's shape by molding with fingers. Cut 1 piece of ¼"-wide coral satin ribbon 3" long. Glue ribbon to inside top edge of box. Wrap dk. apricot 4mm ribbon around each score and secure with glue (see diagram on page 52).

• *Line Box Bottom*

Follow instructions for *"Lining Strips"* on page 12. Glue INSIDE BOTTOM fabric to LINING STRIP. Begin gluing LINING STRIP at any score line to top edge of BOX SIDE.

• *Glue Ribbon Hinge to Inside Lid*

Follow instructions for *"Gluing Ribbon Hinge to Inside Lid"* on page 12.

• *Embellish Box*

Gather 1 short edge of 1"-wide green and gold ombré wired ribbon and secure thread. Turn raw edge under at gathers. Glue gathered edge to box side at center back, ½" up from bottom edge. Extend ribbon to next score. Mark ribbon and gather-stitch across ribbon at mark. Secure thread. Glue gathered ribbon to box side at score, ½" up from bottom edge. Continue to extend ribbon, mark, gather, and glue ribbon around box. Turn raw edge of ribbon under at center back joint, gather, and glue in place.

Turn box upside down. Glue ⅜"-wide lt. green ruffled trim to under-

side edge of box bottom. Glue wrong side of BASE to bottom of box.

Embellish box following instructions below and diagram on page 52.

(A) Stitch 5 ROSETTES with rusty coral 4mm ribbon, using 5" for each . Glue ROSETTE to top edge of draped ribbon at each score line.

(B) Mark center of LID. Puncture LID through cardboard with a needle. Stitch dk. aqua embroidery floss through LID, wrap floss around dip of a scallop, then stitch through LID again. Continue to wrap floss around LID at each scallop until it is completely sectioned with floss.

Following stitch guide and chart on page 52, embroider LID.

Turn LID upside down. FLUTE pale aqua 7mm ribbon while gluing onto underside of LID. FLUTE coral red 7mm ribbon over pale aqua ribbon while gluing onto underside of LID.

Pad LID with 3 layers of batting, then wrap with outer fabric. Glue wrong side of LID to wrong side of MIDDLE LID.

(C) Fold remaining 1"-wide green and gold ombré wired ribbon in half, matching short ends. Stitch ¼" seam. Open ribbon out and gather-stitch along one long edge. Pull gathers as tight as possible. Secure thread. Glue ribbon ruffle to center of LID.

(D) Stitch a ROSETTE with 9" of ¼"-wide coral satin ribbon. Add second ruffle to ROSETTE with 5" of coral red 7mm ribbon. Glue to center of ribbon ruffle.

Tools and Materials

Heavy cardboard–12" x 9"
Lightweight cardboard–12" x 3"
Outer fabric (apricot moiré)–15" x 9"
Inside box fabric (aqua cross dyed
 taffeta)–11" x 9"
Quilt batting–5" x 20"

12" of ¼"-wide coral satin
 ribbon; matching thread
24" of 1"-wide green and gold ombré
 wired ribbon; matching thread
15" of ⅜"-wide lt. green
 ruffled trim
1 yd. each of rusty coral, pale apricot,
 grey green, dk. apricot 4mm ribbon
Dk. aqua embroidery floss
30" of pale aqua 7mm ribbon
40" of coral red 7mm ribbon

Hand sewing needle
Size 3 crewel embroidery
 needle
1" and ½" wooden dowel

Heavy Cardboard	Light Cardboard	Inside Fabric	Outer Fabric
BASE and MIDDLE LID -cut 2 LID INSIDE BOTTOM INSIDE LID	BOX SIDE LINING STRIP	INSIDE BOTTOM + 2½"* INSIDE LID + ¾"*	BOX SIDE + ½"* BASE + ½"* MIDDLE LID + ½"* LID + ¾""*

* See page 8.

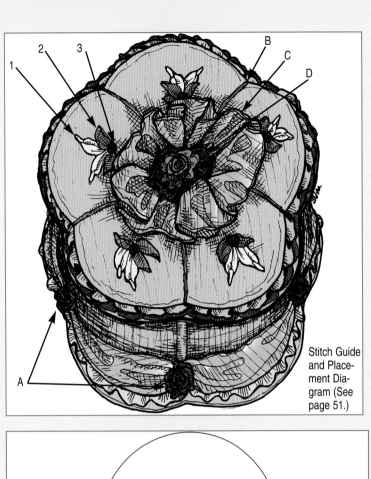

#	*Stitch*	*Ribbon*
1	BULLION LAZY DAISY	Pale apricot 4mm
2	JAPANESE RIBBON STITCH	Grey green 4mm
3	FRENCH KNOTS	Rusty coral 4mm

Stitch Guide and Placement Diagram (See page 51.)

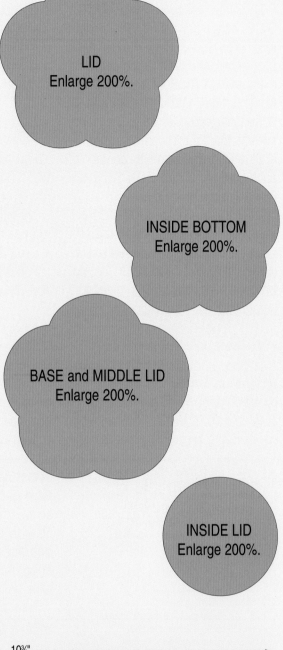

LID
Enlarge 200%.

INSIDE BOTTOM
Enlarge 200%.

BASE and MIDDLE LID
Enlarge 200%.

INSIDE LID
Enlarge 200%.

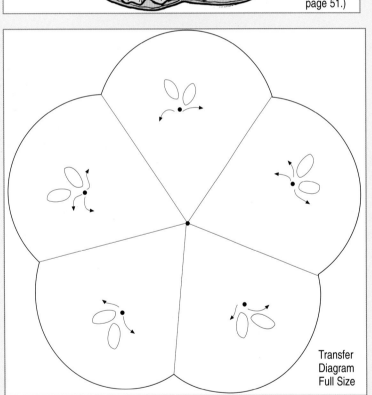

Transfer Diagram Full Size

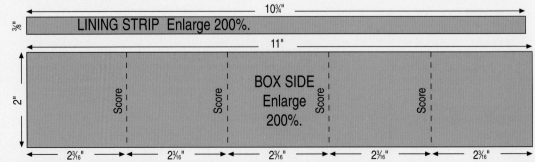

10¾"

LINING STRIP Enlarge 200%.

⅜"

11"

BOX SIDE
Enlarge 200%.

2"

Score   Score   Score   Score

2³⁄₁₆"   2³⁄₁₆"   2³⁄₁₆"   2³⁄₁₆"   2³⁄₁₆"

Patterns reduced to 50% of original. Enlarge 200%.

- *Cut Cardboard, Paper and Fabric, Score*

- *Cover Cardboard with Fabric and Paper*

Laminate unscored side of INSIDE BOX SIDE with accent fabric. Leave 1 short edge unwrapped. Fold at each score mark and emphasize scores.

Pad INSIDE BOTTOM with batting, and wrap with accent fabric.

Pad each OUTSIDE SECTION with batting and wrap with paper. Cut ⅝"-wide ivory French Val lace into 6 pieces, each 6". Gather lace and glue edge to underside top curved edge of each OUTSIDE BOX SECTION, tapering ends.

- *Assemble Box*

Follow instructions for *"Assembling Box Bottom"* of hinge-lid-style boxes on page 12. Slip INSIDE BOTTOM into INSIDE BOX SIDE ¹⁄₁₆" down from narrowest edge. Glue in place with a thin bead of hot glue.

- *Assemble Drawstring Top*

Stitch DRAWSTRING TOP sides with ¼" seam, leaving opening as shown on pattern. Press seam open. Turn and press top edge under ¼". Fold top edge down on fold line. Pin to hold in place. Stitch on casing lines. Cut ⅛"-wide aqua ribbon in half. Thread one-half through casing from side opening. Tie ends together. Thread remaining ribbon through casing from opposite side opening.

Tie ends together. Pull 1 ribbon through casing to hide knots within casing. Repeat with other ribbon. Pull 2 ribbons together to close DRAWSTRING TOP.

Glue ½" of unfinished edge of DRAWSTRING TOP to top edge of INSIDE BOX SIDE, on wrong side, lining DRAWSTRING TOP'S side seams to INSIDE BOX SIDE as shown on pattern.

- *Finish Box*

Glue OUTSIDE BOX SECTIONS to INSIDE BOX SIDE, matching curves. Glue BASE to bottom of box. Trim side edges with turquoise and yellow bud and bow garland and bottom with yellow bud and bow garland.

Tools and Materials

Heavy cardboard–8" x 12"
Lightweight cardboard–15" x 7"
Accent fabric (aqua satin)–9" x 44"
Wrapping paper or decoupage
 paper–12" square
Quilt batting–6" x 10"

1 yd. of ⅝"-wide ivory French Val lace
1 yd. of ⅛"-wide aqua ribbon
1½ yd. of turquoise and yellow bud and
 bow garland
12" of yellow bud and bow garland

Large, blunt needle
1" wooden dowel

Heavy Cardboard	Light Cardboard	Accent Fabric	Paper
INSIDE BOTTOM BASE OUTSIDE BOX SECTION-cut 6	INSIDE BOX SIDE	INSIDE BOTTOM + ½"* INSIDE BOX SIDE + ¾"* DRAWSTRING TOP	BASE + ½"* BASE + ½"* OUTSIDE BOX SECTION + ½"*-cut 6

* See page 8.

INSIDE BOX SIDE pattern reduced to 80% of original. Enlarge 125%. DRAWSTRING TOP reduced to 50% of original. Enlarge 200%. All other patterns full size.

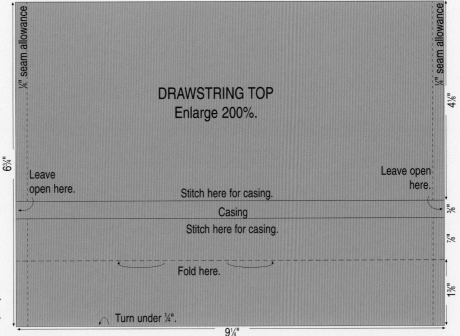

¼" seam allowance

¼" seam allowance

6¾"

4⅛"

DRAWSTRING TOP
Enlarge 200%.

Leave open here.

Leave open here.

Stitch here for casing.

Casing

Stitch here for casing.

⅜"

⅞"

Fold here.

1⅜"

Turn under ¼".

9¼"

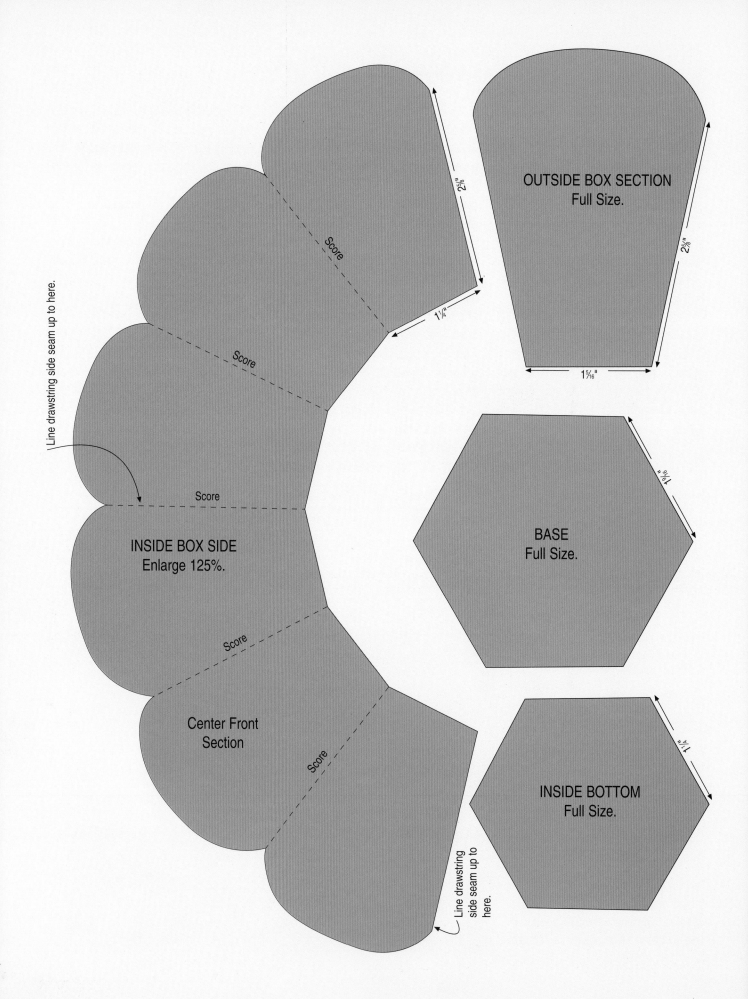

OUTSIDE BOX SECTION
Full Size.

2⅝"

2⅝"

1¼"

1 5/16 "

Score

Score

Line drawstring side seam up to here.

Score

INSIDE BOX SIDE
Enlarge 125%.

Score

Center Front
Section

Score

Line drawstring side seam up to here.

BASE
Full Size.

9/16"

INSIDE BOTTOM
Full Size.

1¼"

• Cut Cardboard and Fabric, Score

Use a rotary cutter and cutting mat on fabric to produce precise, clean cuts.

• Cover Outer Box Jacket with Fabric and Assemble

Glue 2 layers of OUTER BOX JACKET TOP, OUTER BOX JACKET BOTTOM, and OUTER BOX JACKET SIDE together creating 1 top, 1 bottom and 1 side. Place OUTER BOX JACKET fabric wrong side up on work surface. Laminate BOTTOM section ¾" from right edge of fabric and centered. Mark a ⅛" space on left side of BOTTOM. Place and laminate SIDE section at ⅛" mark so bottom edges are lined up. Mark a ⅛" space on left side of SIDE. Place and laminate TOP section at ⅛" mark so bottom edges are lined up. Wrap all edges of fabric onto cardboard. Roll underside of TOP with glue. Center and laminate inside jacket liner fabric onto underside of TOP.

Tools and Materials

Heavy cardboard–32" x 40"
Lightweight cardboard–10" x 14"
Outer fabric (music print cotton)–⅝ yd.
Contrasting fabric (floral print cotton)–¼ yd.
Fusing material– 16" x 3"

27" of ¼"-wide dk. khaki green velvet ribbon
Eight 1" x 3" fabric scraps
1 yd. of ivory tiny picot trim
½ yd. purple 4mm ribbon
½ yd. ivory weavable lace
4" of 1"-wide aqua and brown ombré wired ribbon
24" of lilac and gold 4mm ribbon
24" of ⅜"-wide green iridescent ribbon
2" scrap of rose iridescent fabric
Small mother of pearl buckle
7 musical brass pieces
Old cameo or button

1" wooden dowel
Industrial-strength adhesive
Rotary cutter and cutting mat
Masking tape

• Cover Outer Box with Fabric and Assemble

Laminate unscored side of OUTER BOX with outer fabric. Finish all edges. Fold at each score and emphasize scores. Fold OUTER BOX up at sides and cleanly tape together with masking tape. Roll 2 short sides and 1 long side of outside of OUTER BOX with glue. Laminate contrasting fabric strip onto glued OUTER BOX, placing cut edge ¹⁄₁₆" down from finished top edge. Leave a ¾" tab of contrasting fabric to wrap to remaining long edge. Glue unfinished edge of contrasting fabric to underside of OUTER BOX. Glue underside of OUTER BOX to wrong side of BOTTOM, butting unfinished long edge of OUTER BOX up to left edge of BOTTOM. Glue unfinished side of OUTER BOX to wrong side of SIDE, so TOP closes easily.

Laminate mountain-scored side of OUTER BOX INSIDE DIVIDER with outer fabric. Finish all edges. Fold at mountain score and emphasize score. Turn cardboard wrong side up. Fold at valley scores and emphasize scores. Glue wrong side together in between valley scores, creating a stand-up divider. Glue underside of divider to INSIDE BOTTOM of OUTER BOX.

• Cover Inside Box with Fabric and Assemble

Laminate unscored side of INSIDE BOX with contrasting fabric. Finish all edges. Fold at each score and emphasize scores. Fold up at sides and cleanly tape together with masking tape. Roll outer edge with glue. Laminate contrasting fabric strip onto glued INSIDE BOX, placing cut edge ¹⁄₁₆" down from finished top edge. Overlap ends of fabric ¾" at 1 short side. Glue unfinished edge of strip to underside of INSIDE BOX. Roll bottom with glue. Cover bottom of INSIDE BOX with contrasting fabric.

Laminate mountain-scored side of INSIDE BOX DIVIDER with contrasting fabric. Finish all 4 edges. Fold at mountain score and emphasize score. Turn wrong side up. Fold at valley scores and emphasize scores. Glue wrong side together in between valley scores, creating a stand-up divider. Glue underside of DIVIDER to inside bottom of INSIDE BOX. Place inside box into outer box.

• Embellish Box

Glue ¼"-wide dk. khaki green velvet ribbon to bottom edge of OUTER BOX.

Fuse fabric scraps onto fusing material. Fuse 3" x 8" piece of contrasting fabric onto fusing material. Using pattern on page 60, cut 8 right pointing fabric pieces for star from fused contrasting fabric. From all 8 scraps, cut a left pointing fabric piece. Fuse star onto box top, alternating contrasting fabric and scraps. Glue ivory tiny picot trim over raw edges.

Heavy Cardboard	Light Cardboard	Contrasting Fabric	Outer Fabric
OUTER BOX JACKET TOP and BOTTOM- cut 4 OUTER BOX JACKET SIDE-cut 2 OUTER BOX INSIDE BOX	OUTER BOX INSIDE DIVIDER INSIDE BOX DIVIDER	INSIDE BOX + ½"* INSIDE BOX DIVIDER + ½"* OUTER BOX 24" x 3½" INSIDE BOX 21½" x 2¼" INSIDE BOX BOTTOM 3¾" x 6"	OUTER BOX JACKET 19" x 11" Inside jacket liner 8½" x 8" OUTER BOX + ¾"* OUTER BOX INSIDE DIVIDER + ¾"*

* See page 8.

Weave purple 4mm ribbon through ivory lace. Glue lace around outer edge of star. Seam edges of aqua and brown 1"-wide ombré wired ribbon for a bow. Thread bow through buckle. Glue buckled bow to center of star.

Drape gold and lilac 4mm and green iridescent ⅜"-wide ribbons around top and side edges of box top. Glue in place. Glue brass pieces and cameo where desired with industrial-strength adhesive. From 2" rose iridescent fabric circle, stitch unstuffed GRAPE. Glue in place.

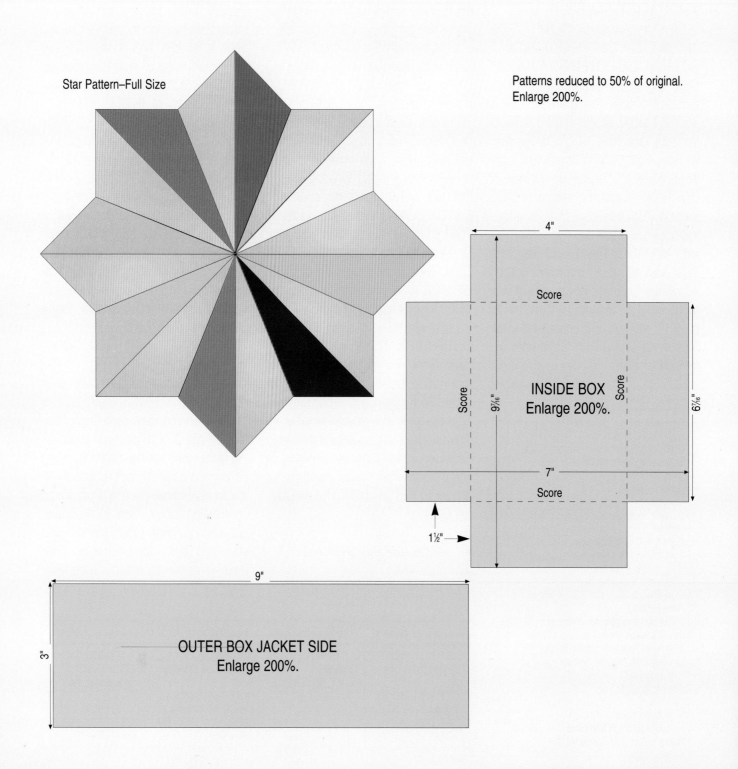

Star Pattern–Full Size

Patterns reduced to 50% of original. Enlarge 200%.

4"

Score

Score   INSIDE BOX   Score
             Enlarge 200%.

9⁷/₁₆"   6⁷/₁₆"

7"

Score

1½"

9"

3"

OUTER BOX JACKET SIDE
Enlarge 200%.

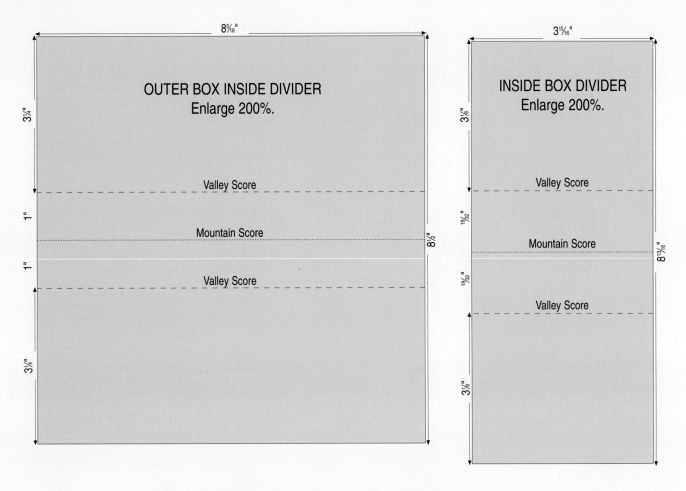

OUTER BOX INSIDE DIVIDER
Enlarge 200%.

8⁵⁄₁₆"

3¼"

Valley Score

1"

Mountain Score

1"

Valley Score

3¼"

8½"

INSIDE BOX DIVIDER
Enlarge 200%.

3¹⁵⁄₁₆"

3⅛"

Valley Score

¹⁹⁄₃₂"

Mountain Score

¹⁹⁄₃₂"

Valley Score

3⅛"

8¹³⁄₁₆"

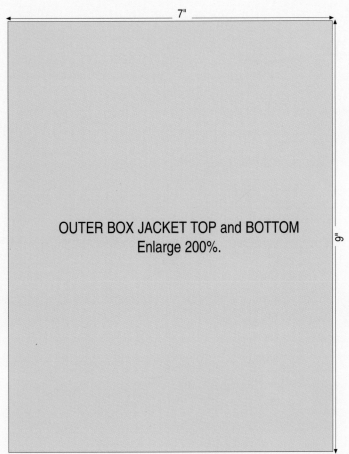

7"

OUTER BOX JACKET TOP and BOTTOM
Enlarge 200%.

9"

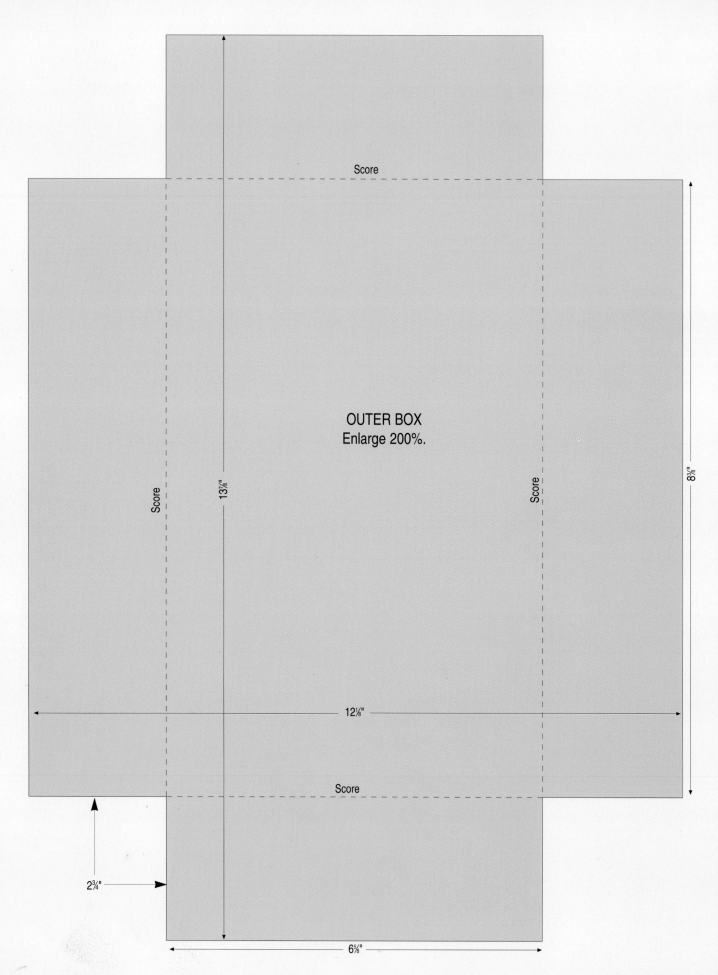

OUTER BOX
Enlarge 200%.

Score

Score

Score

Score

13⅞"

8⅜"

12⅛"

2¾"

6⅝"

• **Cut Cardboard and Fabric, Score**

• **Embroider Framing Front**

Following stitch guide and chart on pages 66 and 67, embroider FRAMING FRONT fabric. Embroider FRAMING FRONT before pad and wrap process.

• **Cover Box Body with Fabric and Assemble**

Laminate unscored side of DRAWER SHELVING with outer fabric, placing fabric where shown on pattern. Wrap fabric around front long edge and 1 short edge. Fold at each score and emphasize scores. Join short edges of each cardboard piece by overlapping finished short edge to tab edge and butting cardboard edges up to each other. Glue tab in place. Fold up and tape back end of DRAWER SHELVING in place with masking tape, creating a compartment to slip drawer into. Repeat for second shelf. Glue DRAWER SHELVINGS together at a side.

Laminate SHELF with outer fabric. Finish all 4 sides. Glue SHELF to top of combined DRAWER SHELVINGS.

• **Cover Framing with Fabric and Assemble**

Laminate scored side of FRAMING with outer fabric. Finish all edges. Fold at scores and emphasize scores. Glue bottom 1" of wrong side of FRAMING to outside of combined DRAWER SHELVINGS with SHELF. Pull cardboard tight for a snug fit, lining up front edges of FRAMING with DRAWER SHELVING.

Pad FRAMING SIDE, 1 left and 1 right, with batting, and wrap with outer fabric. Pad FRAMING FRONT with batting and wrap with outer fabric. Glue wrong side of FRAMING SIDES to wrong side of FRAMING at sides, lining up all edges. Glue wrong side of FRAMING FRONT to wrong side of FRAMING at back, lining up all edges.

Laminate BASE with outer fabric. Finish all 4 sides. Glue wrong side of BASE to underside of DRAWER SHELVINGS. Glue lt. blue narrow cording in between SHELF and DRAWER SHELVING, around top edge of FRAMING, and at BASE of box.

• **Cover Drawers with Fabric and Assemble**

Fold DRAWER up at scores and tape corners together. Roll outside edge of drawer with glue. Cover with DRAWER strip so ½" of inside fabric extends past bottom of DRAWER. Smooth fabric completely. Overlap fabric at 1 long edge ¾". Paint inside edge and ¾" of inside bottom of each DRAWER with glue. Wrap fabric strip to inside, clipping at corners.

Laminate and wrap inside fabric onto each DRAWER BASE and LINER. Glue wrong side of LINER to inside of DRAWER. Turn upside down. Fold a 2" pieces of lt. blue 7mm ribbon in half. Glue ribbon at center front edge. Glue wrong side of DRAWER BASE to underside of DRAWER. Repeat all steps for second drawer.

Laminate DRAWER FRONTS with outer fabric. Glue DRAWER FRONTS onto drawers, lining up bottom edges, and centering between sides. Slip drawers into drawer shelving.

• **Assemble Pincushion**

Fold pincushion fabric strip in half, matching short edges. Stitch ¼" seam at short edges. Press seam open. Glue ¼" of long edge of seamed fabric to bottom edge of PINCUSHION. Firmly stuff fabric with Polyfill. Gather-

---

Tools and Materials

Heavy cardboard–12" x 30"
Lightweight cardboard–16" x 16"
Outer fabric (lightweight ivory brocade)–⅜ yd.
Inside fabric, pincushion fabric (lt. blue oriental print satin)–8" x 22"
Quilt batting–20" x 6"

1½ yd. lt. blue narrow cording
1 yd. each of lime, apricot, rose, blue, aqua and grey 7mm ribbon or 2½ yds. variegated ribbon
1 yd. each of bright rose, yellow, grey, olive, green, purple, pink, peach and blue 4mm ribbon
⅝ yd. each of ¹⁄₁₆"-wide lt. and med. blue, and lt. green ribbons
½ yd. of lt. blue 7mm ribbon
One handful Polyfill
1 yd. white embroidery floss
Button for pincushion center

Large needle
Size 3 crewel embroidery needle
Masking tape
1" dowel

Heavy Cardboard	Light Cardboard	Inside Fabric	Outer Fabric
FRAMING	DRAWER SHELVING -cut 2	DRAWER strip 17½" x 2" -cut 2	FRAMING + ½"*
FRAMING FRONT	DRAWER BASE-cut 2	DRAWER BASE + ½"* -cut 2	FRAMING SIDES + ½"*-cut 2
FRAMING SIDE-cut 2	LINER-cut 2	LINER + ½"*-cut 2	SHELF + ½"*
SHELF		PINCUSHION BASE + ½"*	BASE + ½"*
BASE		PINCUSHION 7½" x 2"	DRAWER FRONT + ½"*-cut 2
DRAWER-cut 2			FRAMING FRONT + ¾"*
DRAWER FRONT-cut 2			DRAWER SHELVING 9½" x 3"-cut 2
PINCUSHION			
PINCUSHION BASE			

* See page 8.

stitch top edge of fabric. Pull stitches as tight as possible and secure thread.

Sculpt center of pincushion by taking thread down center and through cardboard, and back up, down and up again. Use large needle. Pull thread tight each time to indent center of pincushion. Wrap white embroidery floss around outer edge of pin-cushion, then through center 8 times to section. Pull floss tight to sculpt sides of pincushion. Sew button to top of pincushion at center of wraps.

Turn upside down. FLUTE lt. blue 7mm ribbon while gluing onto bottom of pincushion. Laminate PINCUSHION BASE with inside fabric. Glue BASE to bottom of pincushion. Glue pincushion to SHELF at center back.

Tie a knot in the center of $\frac{1}{16}$"-wide med. and lt. blue and lt. green ribbons. Glue to center back of box. Cascade down both sides, knotting occasionally (see diagram below) and securing with glue. Knot ends of tails.

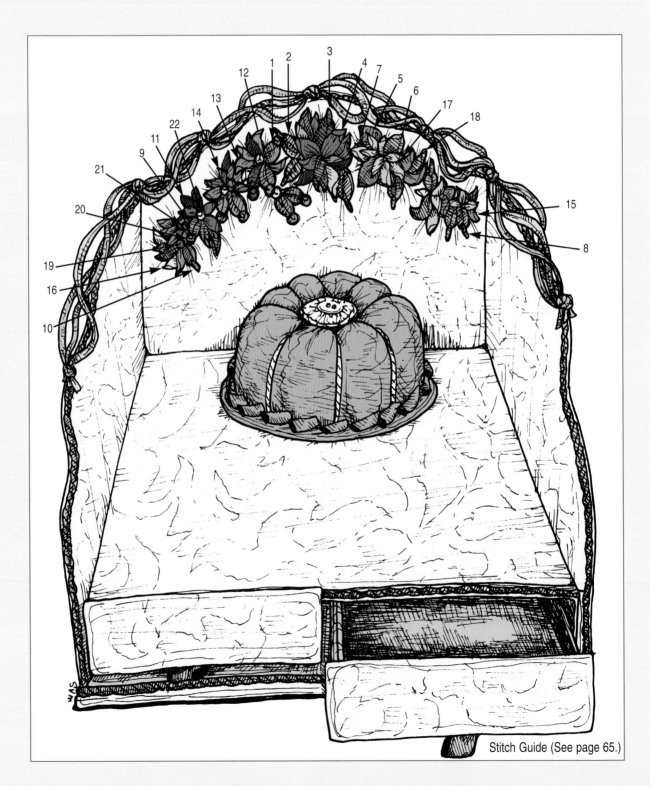

Stitch Guide (See page 65.)

#	Stitch	Ribbon
1	KNOTTED LAZY DAISY	Apricot 7mm
2	BULLION LAZY DAISY	Lime 7mm
3	BULLION LAZY DAISY	Rose 7mm
4	JAPANESE RIBBON STITCH	Rose 7mm
5	JAPANESE RIBBON STITCH	Blue 7mm
6	JAPANESE RIBBON STITCH	Aqua 7mm
7	JAPANESE RIBBON STITCH	Grey 7mm
8	BULLION LAZY DAISY	Green 4mm
9	BULLION LAZY DAISY	Peach 4mm
10	BULLION LAZY DAISY	Blue 4mm
11	JAPANESE RIBBON STITCH	Bright rose 4mm
12	JAPANESE RIBBON STITCH	Purple 4mm
13	JAPANESE RIBBON STITCH	Pink 4mm
14	JAPANESE RIBBON STITCH	Peach 4mm
15	JAPANESE RIBBON STITCH	Blue 4mm
16	JAPANESE RIBBON STITCH	Yellow 4mm
17	JAPANESE RIBBON STITCH	Grey 4mm
18	JAPANESE RIBBON STITCH	Olive 4mm
19	FRENCH KNOT	Bright rose 4mm
20	FRENCH KNOT	Blue 4mm
21	FRENCH KNOT	Olive 4mm
22	FRENCH KNOT	Yellow 4mm

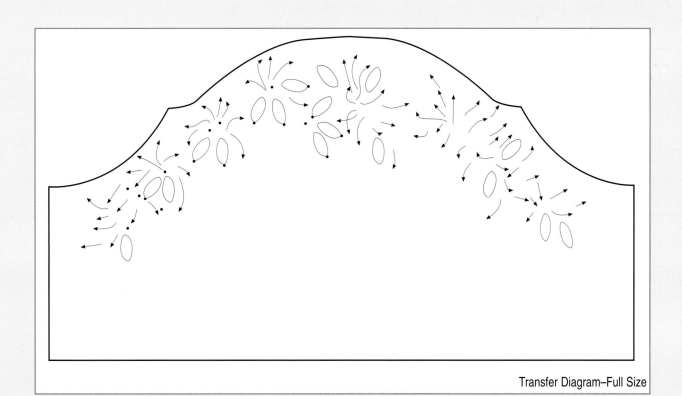

Transfer Diagram–Full Size

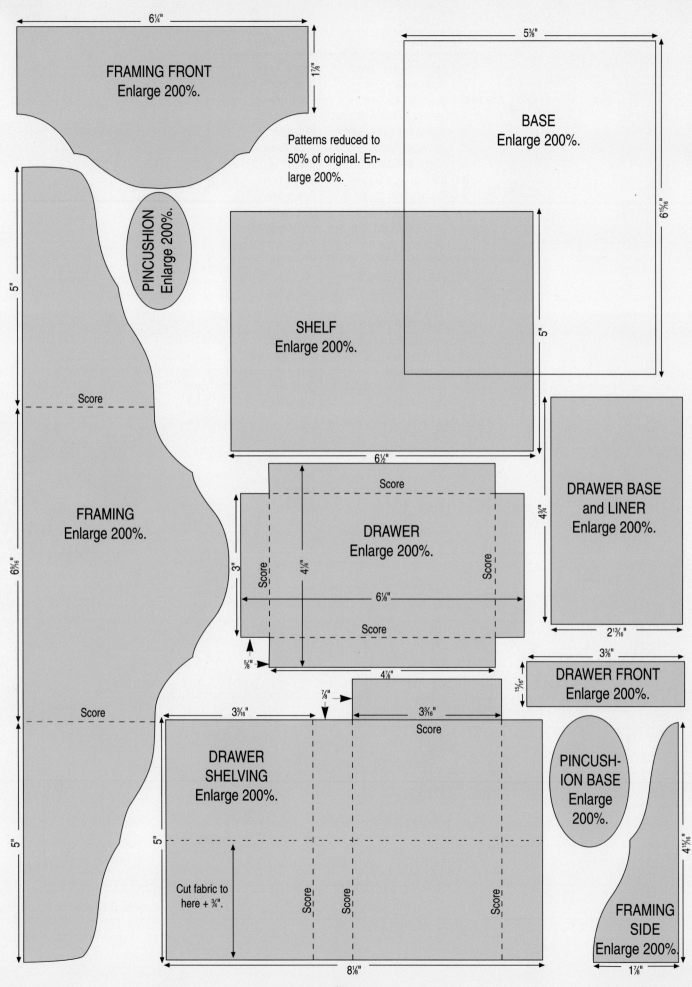

FRAMING FRONT
Enlarge 200%.

6¼"

1⅞"

BASE
Enlarge 200%.

5⅜"

6¹⁵⁄₁₆"

Patterns reduced to
50% of original. En-
large 200%.

PINCUSHION
Enlarge 200%.

SHELF
Enlarge 200%.

5"

5"

6½"

Score

FRAMING
Enlarge 200%.

5"

6⁹⁄₁₆"

DRAWER
Enlarge 200%.

Score

Score

Score

Score

3"

4¼"

6⅛"

4⅞"

5⅞"

DRAWER BASE
and LINER
Enlarge 200%.

4¾"

2¹³⁄₁₆"

3⅜"

DRAWER FRONT
Enlarge 200%.

¹⁵⁄₁₆"

Score

7⁄8"

3³⁄₁₆"

3³⁄₁₆"

Score

Score

DRAWER
SHELVING
Enlarge 200%.

5"

5"

Cut fabric to
here + ¾".

Score

Score

Score

8⅛"

PINCUSH-
ION BASE
Enlarge
200%.

FRAMING
SIDE
Enlarge 200%.

4¹⁵⁄₁₆"

1⅞"

68

• Cut Cardboard and Fabric, Score

• Cover Cardboard with Fabric and Shape

Laminate unscored side of BOX SIDE with outer fabric. Place right side up on work surface. Fold at each score mark and emphasize scores. Place wrong side up on work surface. Carefully roll with ½" dowel in between each score and next to outer scores. Use INSIDE BOTTOM as a guide for shape. Re-roll each scallop with ¼" dowel for added shape. Stand BOX SIDE up. Pinch at each score mark. Place right side up on work surface. Roll with ½" dowel to fit indented side of box.

Laminate BASE and MIDDLE LID with outer fabric. Pad LID with 3 layers of batting, then wrap with outer fabric. Pad INSIDE LID with 1 layer of batting, then wrap with inside fabric. INSIDE BOTTOM is not wrapped with fabric.

• Assemble Box Bottom

Follow instructions for *"Assembling Box Bottom"* of hinge-lid-style boxes on page 12. Begin gluing in place at a matching scallop. Hold until dry. Continue to glue INSIDE BOTTOM to BOX SIDE, 1 scallop at a time, matching each score line with dip of each scallop. Overlap and glue BOX SIDE'S finished edges at center back. Emphasize clam shell's shape by molding at curves and pinching at dips. Cut 2 pieces of ⅜"-wide peach satin ribbon. Glue ribbons to inside top edge of box ½" from center back.

• Line Box Bottom

Follow instructions for *"Lining Strips"* of hinge-lid-style boxes on page 12. Glue INSIDE BOTTOM fabric onto LINING STRIP. Mold box shape with fingers while gluing LINING STRIP in place. Pinch box side of scallop dips again to emphasize clam-shell shape. Glue mauve narrow soutache braid to inside top edge of box. Stitch inside lining fabric through box bottom for texture. Stitch large pearl at center back of box bottom. Tie a bow using 5 different 4mm ribbons. Glue bow to inside center front of box bottom. Knot ends of ribbons.

• Attach Ribbon Hinge to Inside Lid

Follow instructions for *"Gluing Ribbon Hinge to Inside Lid"* on page 12.

• Embellish Box

Turn box upside down. FLUTE ¼"-wide ivory velvet ribbon while gluing onto underside of box. Glue wrong side of BASE to bottom of box.

Mark LID at center back dot for tufting (see diagram on page 72). Puncture LID through cardboard with large, blunt needle. Knot and stitch golden brown very narrow cording through puncture, around first scallop, then through underside of LID again. Pull cording tight so batting indents slightly, but do not buckle cardboard. Continue to wrap narrow cording around LID at each scallop until it is completely sectioned with cording. Glue cording on underside of LID.

Mark placement for cameo with disappearing pen. Stitch through cardboard at marks with quilting thread to create an indented place for cameo. Weave pale peach 4mm ribbon through ivory narrow lace, then glue lace at outer edge of stitching on box top. Glue cameo in place.

Tie tiny bow with ivory and ecru 4mm ribbon. Glue bow in place. Cascade tails. Glue wrong side of LID to MIDDLE LID.

Glue ivory narrow tatting to outer edge of LID.

Tools and Materials

Heavy cardboard–15" x 25"
Lightweight cardboard–3" x 22"
Outer fabric (apricot damask)–⅓ yd.
Inside fabric (coral chiffon)–12" x 22"
Quilt batting–¼ yd.

6" of ⅜"-wide peach satin ribbon
22" of mauve narrow soutache braid
½ yd. each of 5 different shades 4mm ribbon
1½ yd. of ¼"-wide ivory velvet ribbon
2½ yds. of golden brown very narrow cording
6" of ivory narrow weavable lace
9" of pale peach 4mm ribbon
½ yd. each of ivory and ecru 4mm ribbon
22" of ivory narrow tatting
Cameo or other favorite piece
1 large pearl

Large, blunt needle
Size 3 crewel embroidery needle
Quilting thread
Disappearing pen
1", ½" and ¼" wooden dowels

Heavy Cardboard	Light Cardboard	Inside Fabric	Outer Fabric
INSIDE BOTTOM	LINING STRIP	INSIDE BOTTOM + 1¾"*	BASE and MIDDLE
BASE and MIDDLE LID -cut 2	BOX SIDE	INSIDE LID + ¾"*	LID + ½"*-cut 2
LID			LID + ¾"*
INSIDE LID			BOX SIDE + ½"*

* See page 8.

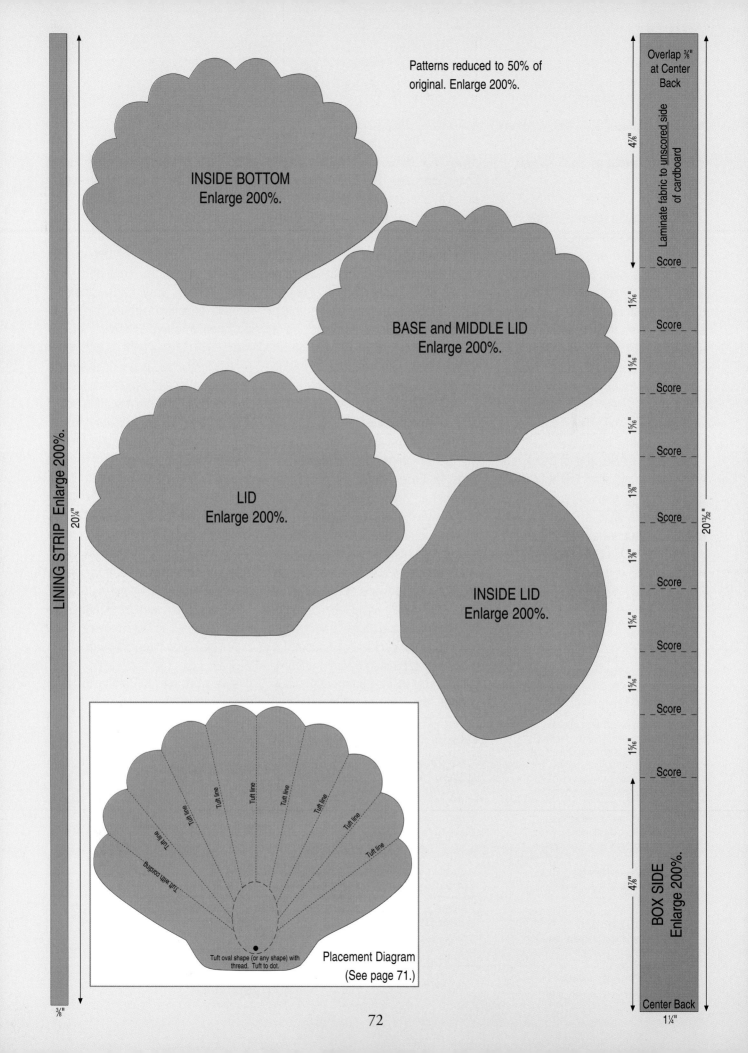

Patterns reduced to 50% of original. Enlarge 200%.

LINING STRIP Enlarge 200%.

20¼"

⅜"

INSIDE BOTTOM
Enlarge 200%.

BASE and MIDDLE LID
Enlarge 200%.

LID
Enlarge 200%.

INSIDE LID
Enlarge 200%.

Overlap ⅜"
at Center
Back

Laminate fabric to unscored side
of cardboard

4⅞"

Score

1⁵⁄₁₆"

Score

1⁵⁄₁₆"

Score

1⁵⁄₁₆"

Score

1⅜"

Score

1⅜"

Score

1⁵⁄₁₆"

Score

1⁵⁄₁₆"

Score

1⁵⁄₁₆"

Score

4⅞"

20¹³⁄₃₂"

BOX SIDE
Enlarge 200%.

Center Back

1¼"

Tuft line

Tuft line

Tuft line

Tuft line

Tuft line

Tuft line

Tuft line

Tuft line

Tuft with cording

Tuft oval shape (or any shape) with
thread. Tuft to dot.

Placement Diagram
(See page 71.)

72

• *Cut Cardboard and Fabric, Score*

• *Cover Cardboard with Fabric, Shape and Assemble*

Outside Box: Laminate unscored side of OUTSIDE BOX A with outer fabric. Place unscored side up on work surface. Fold at each score mark and emphasize scores. Roll back end with ½" dowel. Fold at scores for assembly. Glue overlap onto side edge. Flatten glue. Masking-tape back end strip to top and bottom edge of back end for a snug fit.

Laminate scored side of OUTSIDE BOX SIDE A with outer fabric. Finish all edges. Shape like OUTSIDE BOX A. Glue OUTSIDE BOX SIDE to OUTSIDE BOX. Turn upside down. FLUTE ¼"-wide lt. gold satin ribbon while gluing onto underside of box.

Laminate OUTSIDE BOX BOTTOM A with outer fabric. Finish all edges. Glue wrong side of BOTTOM to bottom of box.

Inside Box: Fold INSIDE BOX B at each score mark and emphasize

scores. Roll back end and front end strips with ½" dowel to shape. Fold box at scores for assembly. Masking-tape back end strip to bottom edge of back end for a snug fit. Repeat for front end. Tape remaining edges together for a snug fit. Laminate INSIDE BOX strip to outside sides. Wrap unfinished fabric edges to bottom of box and inside top edge of box.

Laminate INSIDE BOX BASE B with inside fabric. Finish all edges. Glue wrong side of BASE B to INSIDE BOX B bottom.

Inside Box Liner: Pad INSIDE BOTTOM C with 1 layer of batting and wrap with surprise fabric. Glue wrong side of INSIDE BOTTOM C to inside of INSIDE BOX B.

Laminate unscored side of INSIDE BOX LINER INSIDE SIDE C with surprise fabric. Finish 2 long edges and 1 short edge. Place right side up on work surface. Fold at each score and mark and emphasize scores. Roll each end with ½" dowel. Join short edges of INSIDE SIDE C by overlap-

ping finished short edge to tab edge, and butting cardboard edges up to each other. Glue in place. Slip INSIDE SIDE C into INSIDE BOX B. Glue in place. Embroider OUTSIDE BOX TOP A fabric before pad and wrap process.

• *Embellish and Embroider Box*

Cut out printed silk to fit onto OUTSIDE BOX TOP A fabric. Position silk on one side and place lace scraps over edges. Position other laces as in diagram. Embroider fabric and lace in place following stitch guide and chart on page 77.

Stitch 7 ROSETTES with dk. rose 4mm ribbon. Set aside.

Pad and wrap embellished BOX TOP A fabric to OUTSIDE BOX TOP A. Glue to box top.

(A) Glue ribbon ROSETTES to box top as shown in diagram on page 77.

Glue narrow gold cording around top and front side edges of box.

Tools and Materials
Heavy cardboard–9" x 14"
Lightweight cardboard–20" x 20"
Outer fabric (lt. gold lamé)–18" x 14"
Inside fabric (gold jacquard)–7" x 20"
Surprise fabric (green velvet)–18" x 7"
Printed silk, or something with a similar look
Quilt batting–8' square
54" of ¼"-wide lt. gold satin ribbon
5"-lengths of 6 scraps of narrow lace edgings
Dk., and lt. rose; red, dk. pink, olive green, lt. green and blue green 4mm silk ribbon; matching thread
1 yd. olive green embroidery floss
27" of narrow gold cording
Hand sewing needle
Size 3 crewel embroidery needle
1" and ½" dowel
Masking tape

Heavy Cardboard	Light Cardboard	Inside Fabric	Outer Fabric
OUTSIDE BOX TOP A	OUTSIDE BOX A	INSIDE BOX strip 2¾" x 18½"	OUTSIDE BOX SIDE A + ½"*
OUTSIDE BOX BOTTOM A	OUTSIDE BOX SIDE A	INSIDE BOX BASE B + ½"*	OUTSIDE BOX TOP A + ¾"*
INSIDE BOX BASE B	INSIDE BOX B		OUTSIDE BOX BOTTOM A + ¾"*
INSIDE BOX LINER INSIDE BOTTOM C	INSIDE BOX LINER INSIDE SIDE C	**Surprise Fabric**	OUTSIDE BOX + ½"*
		INSIDE BOX LINER INSIDE SIDE C + ½"*	(to dotted line)
		INSIDE BOX LINER INSIDE BOTTOM C + ½"*	

* See page 8.

#	Stitch	Ribbon or Floss
1	Couching Stitch	3 strands of olive green floss
2	Bullion Lazy Daisy	Red 4mm ribbon
3	Bullion Lazy Daisy	Dk. rose 4mm ribbon
4	Japanese Ribbon Stitch	Dk. rose 4mm ribbon
5	Japanese Ribbon Stitch	Dk. pink 4mm ribbon
6	Japanese Ribbon Stitch	Lt. rose 4mm ribbon
7	Japanese Ribbon Stitch	Olive green 4mm ribbon
8	Japanese Ribbon Stitch	Blue green 4mm ribbon
9	Lazy Daisy	Lt. green 4mm ribbon

4 Stitch Guide and Placement Diagram (See page 75.)

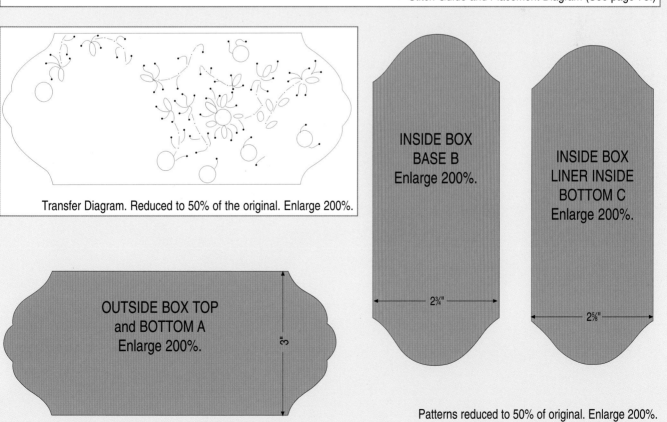

Transfer Diagram. Reduced to 50% of the original. Enlarge 200%.

INSIDE BOX
BASE B
Enlarge 200%.

INSIDE BOX
LINER INSIDE
BOTTOM C
Enlarge 200%.

OUTSIDE BOX TOP
and BOTTOM A
Enlarge 200%.

3"

2¾"

2⅝"

Patterns reduced to 50% of original. Enlarge 200%.

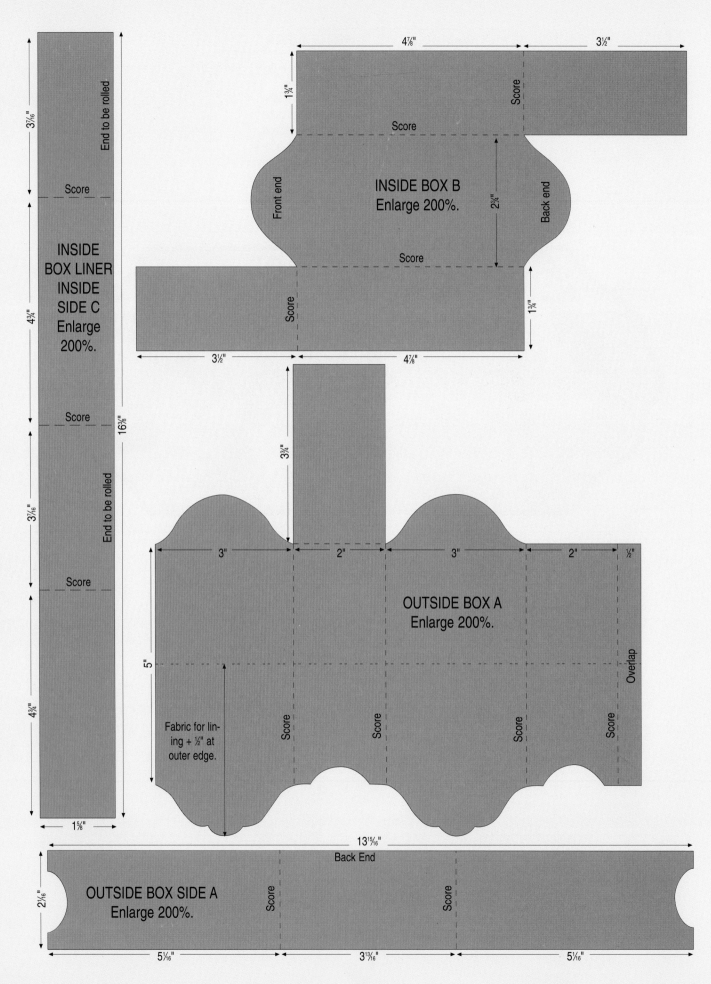

INSIDE BOX LINER INSIDE SIDE C Enlarge 200%.

End to be rolled
Score
Score
Score
End to be rolled

3⁷/₁₆"
4³/₄"
3⁷/₁₆"
4³/₄"

16⅜"
1⅝"

INSIDE BOX B Enlarge 200%.

4⅞"
3½"
1¾"
Score
Score
Front end
Back end
2¾"
1¾"
Score
3½"
4⅞"

OUTSIDE BOX A Enlarge 200%.

3¾"
3"
2"
3"
2"
½"
5"
Overlap
Fabric for lining + ½" at outer edge.
Score
Score
Score
Score

OUTSIDE BOX SIDE A Enlarge 200%.

13¹⁵/₁₆"
Back End
2¹/₁₆"
Score
Score
5¹/₁₆"
3¹³/₁₆"
5¹/₁₆"

• *Cut Cardboard and Fabric, Score*

• *Cover Cardboard with Fabric and Shape*

Laminate INSIDE BOX SIDE with inside fabric. Leave 1 short edge unwrapped. Laminate OUTSIDE BOX SIDE with outer fabric. Finish all 4 sides.

Place OUTSIDE BOX SIDE wrong side up on work surface. Fold at score mark and emphasize score. Carefully roll with 1" dowel, beginning at outer short edge and rolling toward center score. Repeat process with INSIDE BOX SIDE, placing right side up on work surface.

Tools and Materials

Heavy cardboard–18" x 30"
Lightweight cardboard–12" x 30"
Outer fabric (lightly quilted ivory fabric)–⅓ yd.
Inside fabric (ivory jacquard)–¼ yd.
Lid base fabric (muslin)–10" square
Five 3" x 5" ivory scraps of fabric–e.g., velvet, satin, lamé, jacquard
Quilt batting–¼ yd.

½ yd. of ⅝"-wide ivory satin ribbon
¾ yd. of ¼"-wide ivory velvet ribbon
½ yd. of 1½"-wide ivory wired ribbon
¾ yd. of ½"-wide scroll gimp
Fifteen 1" squares of assorted ivory fabrics–e.g., velvet, satin, dupioni
Two ¾" squares ivory jacquard
2½" x 7½" ivory and gold jacquard
2" x 6" gold lamé
3" x 45" silver satin
10" of ⅝"-wide ivory wired ribbon
5" of ⅝"-wide grey wired ribbon
1 yd. of ¼"-wide beige satin ribbon
1 yd. of ivory textured 7mm ribbon
12" of ½"-wide pale aqua ribbon
½ yd. of ½"-wide pale pink ribbon
5" of ½"-wide beige ribbon
3" x 9" beige fabric
¾ yd. of 1½"-wide ivory satin ribbon
¾ yd. of pale green textured 7mm ribbon
5" of lt. brown textured 7mm ribbon
22" of ⅝"-wide pale green wired ribbon
2 large pearls
1 antique button

Hand sewing needle
1" wooden dowel

Laminate BASE and MIDDLE LID with outer fabric.

Pad INSIDE BOTTOM with 1 layer of batting, then wrap with inside fabric. Pad INSIDE LID with 3 layers of batting and wrap with inside fabric.

Piece outer edges only of muslin (LID) with 5 ivory scraps crazy-quilt style, turning under raw edges of scraps. Center section will be completely covered with other decorations. Pad LID with 1 layer of batting and wrap with pieced fabric.

• *Assemble Box*

Follow instructions for *"Assembling Box Bottom"* of flask-style boxes on page 12. Remember this box has a ribbon hinge! Begin gluing at center front. Before finishing gluing at center back, join short edges to tab edge, and butt cardboard edges up to each other. Glue tab in place. Cut ⅝"-wide ivory satin ribbon in half. Glue edge of each ribbon to wrong side of INSIDE BOX SIDE top edge 2½" from center back. When gluing OUTSIDE BOX SIDE to INSIDE BOX SIDE, keep ribbon hinge extended out from box.

When 2 sides are glued together, make back strip. First, press long edges of 2" x 7" strip of outer fabric so long raw edges meet at center of strip. Then glue pressed strip over cardboard edges at center back, leaving 1" at bottom edge to glue to wrong side of box bottom, and 1" to glue to inside top edge. Tuck raw edges at top of strip in between INSIDE BOX SIDE and OUTSIDE BOX SIDE at top edge.

Follow instructions for *"Gluing Ribbon Hinge to Inside Lid"* of hinge-lid-style boxes on page 12. Glue ¼"-wide ivory velvet ribbon to top outer edge of MIDDLE LID. Glue wrong side of LID to wrong side of MIDDLE LID.

Glue wrong side of BASE to bottom of box. Trim bottom edge with 1½"-wide ivory wired ribbon. Tuck raw edges of ribbon under fabric strip at center back of box. Glue ½"-wide scroll gimp to bottom edge of box.

• *Embellish Box*

Embellish LID following instructions below and diagram on page 81.

(A) Make 15 GRAPES from fifteen 1" squares of assorted ivory fabrics and two ¾" squares of ivory jacquard.

(B) Make 2 TURBANS from 2½" x 7½" ivory and gold jacquard and 2" x 6" gold lamé.

(C) Make 1 POINTED PETAL FLOWER from 3" x 45" silver satin.

(D) Make 2 GATHERED LEAVES with ⅝"-wide ivory wired ribbon, using 5" for each leaf. Make 1 GATHERED LEAF with ⅝"-wide grey wired ribbon.

(E) Make 11 FOLDED PETALS with ¼"-wide beige satin ribbon. Gather-stitch all 11 petals together in a chain. Pull thread tight to gather and secure thread for half a flower.

(F) Cut 12 lengths from ivory textured 7mm ribbon, each 3"-long. Tie knot at center of each length of rib-

Heavy Cardboard	Light Cardboard	Inside Fabric	Outer Fabric
INSIDE LID INSIDE BOTTOM LID BASE and MIDDLE LID	INSIDE BOX SIDE OUTSIDE BOX SIDE	INSIDE BOX SIDE + ¾"* INSIDE BOTTOM + ¾"* INSIDE LID + ¾"* **Muslin** LID + ¾"*	OUTSIDE BOX SIDE + ¾"* BASE + ½"* MIDDLE LID + ½"* 2" x 7"

* See page 8.

bon. Fold each length in half, matching short edges, while gather-stitching all 12 petals together in a chain. Pull thread tight to gather and secure thread for a flower.

(G) Make 4 FOLDED PETALS with ½"-wide pale aqua ribbon. Stitch ends in place.

(H) Make 4 ROSETTES, 3 from ½"-wide pale pink ribbon and 1 from ½"-wide beige ribbon.

(I) Press long edges of 3" x 9" beige fabric into thirds. Fold 3 FOLDED LEAVES. Gather-stitch each leaf and secure thread.

Glue all embellishments to LID.

(J) Gather 1½"-wide ivory satin ribbon and glue next to embellishments.

(K) Tie bow with pale green textured 7mm ribbon. Glue bow in place and drape tails. Tack tails in place, using hand sewing needle. Drape lt.

brown textured 7mm ribbon to left of pale green ribbon. Glue pearls to center of turbans and button to center of pointed petal flower (C).

Fold and stitch a 4" looped bow with tails using ⅝"-wide pale green wired ribbon. Glue bow to inside box at center back top edge.

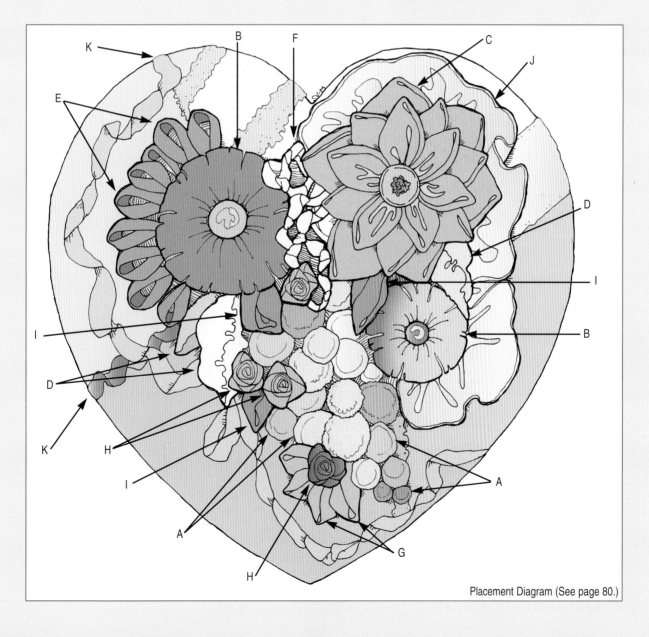

Placement Diagram (See page 80.)

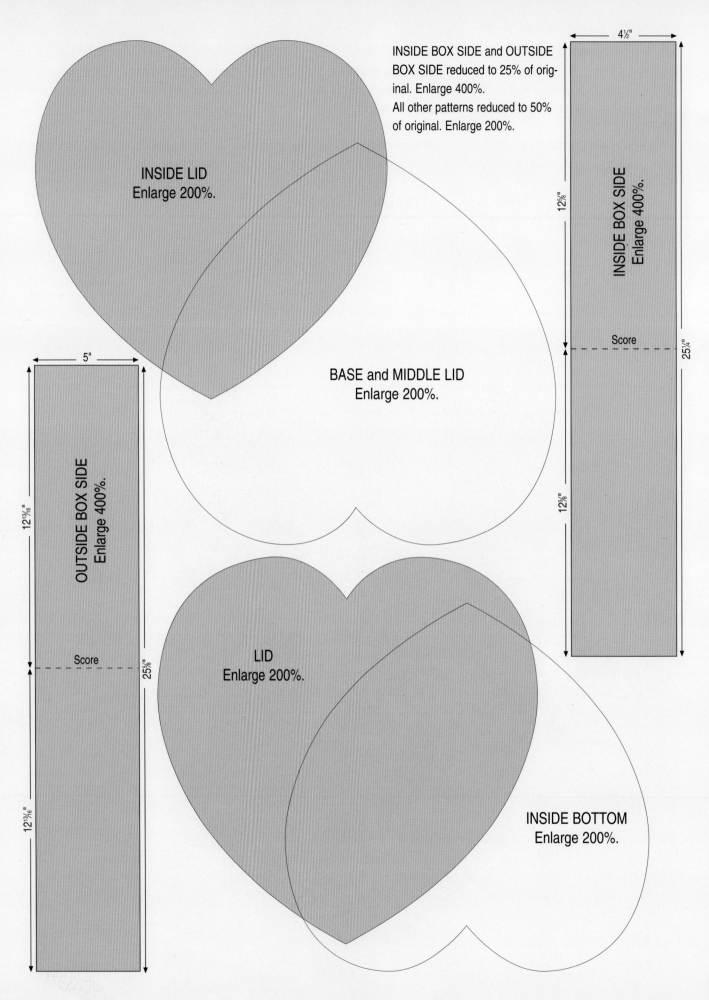

INSIDE LID
Enlarge 200%.

INSIDE BOX SIDE and OUTSIDE
BOX SIDE reduced to 25% of original. Enlarge 400%.
All other patterns reduced to 50%
of original. Enlarge 200%.

4½"

INSIDE BOX SIDE
Enlarge 400%.

12⅝"

Score

25¼"

12⅝"

BASE and MIDDLE LID
Enlarge 200%.

5"

OUTSIDE BOX SIDE
Enlarge 400%.

12¹³⁄₁₆"

Score

25⅝"

LID
Enlarge 200%.

12¹³⁄₁₆"

INSIDE BOTTOM
Enlarge 200%.

82

ANTIQUE *Magical* Victorian

Chapter three

Unexpected

• Cut Cardboard and Fabric, Score

• Cover Inside Cardboard with Fabric, Assemble and Embroider

Laminate unscored side of INSIDE SIDE with inside fabric. Finish 2 long edges and 1 short edge. Fold at each score and emphasize scores. Overlap finished short edge to tab edge and butt cardboard edges up to each other. Glue tab in place.

Laminate INSIDE BOTTOM with inside fabric. Working upside down, slip INSIDE BOTTOM into INSIDE SIDE ¹⁄₁₆" down from edge and glue in place.

Laminate INSIDE TOP and INSIDE TOP SIDES with inside fabric. Place INSIDE TOP right side up on work surface. Roll 9"-long edge of INSIDE TOP with 1" dowel to shape. Glue wrong sides of one 8½"-long edge to curved edge of INSIDE TOP SIDE, right sides together, matching up corners. Glue opposite 8½" edge to curved edge of remaining INSIDE TOP SIDE, right sides together, matching up corners.

Following stitch guide and chart on pages 88 and 89, embroider LID fabric. Use large darning needle for 7mm textured ribbons. Embroider LID fabric before pad and wrap process.

• Cover Outside Cardboard with Fabric and Assemble

Roll each 9¼"-long edge of both OUTSIDE TOP with 1" dowel. Glue 2 layers of rolled OUTSIDE TOPS together, matching up 9¼"-long edges. With masking tape, tape one 9"-long edge to curved edge of OUTSIDE TOP SIDE, matching up corners. Tape opposite 9"-long edge to curved edge of remaining OUTSIDE TOP SIDE, matching up corners.

Center and laminate embroidered top fabric to curved OUTSIDE TOP. Finish front and back edges, eliminating any bulk. Pull remaining sides of fabric around OUTSIDE TOP SIDES, pleating fabric slightly to fit. Wrap raw edges to underside, eliminating any bulk.

Glue 2 sections of OUTSIDE SIDE (FRONT and BACK) together for each front and back. Glue 2 sections of OUTSIDE SIDE (LEFT and RIGHT) together for each left and right side. Place OUTSIDE SIDE fabric wrong side up on work surface. Place BACK ¾" from right edge of strip and centered, laminate. Mark a ⅛" space on left side of BACK. Place LEFT section at mark, long edges lined up, laminate. Mark a ⅛" space on left side of LEFT. Place FRONT section at mark, long edges lined up, laminate. Mark a ⅛" space on left side of FRONT. Place RIGHT section at mark, long edges lined up, laminate. Finish 2 long edges and 1 short edge.

Beginning at tabbed section, glue OUTSIDE SIDE to INSIDE SIDE, wrong sides together, lining up bottom edges. Glue tab over onto 6"-long section of INSIDE SIDE. Continue to glue OUTSIDE SIDE completely around INSIDE SIDE. Pull cardboard tight for a snug fit and use a lot of glue.

Glue 2 BASES together. Laminate combined BASE with outer fabric. Glue wrong side of BASE to bottom of box.

• Embellish and Finish Box

Glue 2"-wide rust ribbon to BOX SIDE at bottom edge. Finish off short edge, overlap and glue onto opposite short edge. Glue black narrow trim to top edge of 2"-wide rust ribbon. Glue dark fancy cording to BASE edge.

Mark center front edge of box top. Gather-stitch center of 2"-wide rust ribbon. Glue gathered center to center mark on box top. Drape ribbon across top and down each side. Glue to underside edge of each OUTSIDE TOP SIDE. Glue black narrow trim to top edge of 2"-wide rust ribbon.

Tools and Materials

Heavy cardboard–32" x 40"
Outer fabric (brown tweed)–½ yd.
Inside fabric (tapestry)–½ yd.

1¼ yd. ¼-wide rust satin ribbon
1½ yd. burgundy 7mm ribbon
1½ yd. burgundy textured 7mm ribbon
½ yd. hunter green 7mm ribbon
¾ yd. olive green 7mm ribbon
1½ yd. burgundy 2mm grosgrain
1 yd. each gold, dk. purple, teal, burgundy, red and hunter green 4mm ribbon or 2 yds. variegated ribbon
1 yd. ¼"-wide of black cording
1 yd. dark fancy cording
2½ yds. of black narrow trim
1½ yds. of 2"-wide rust ribbon
9" of ⅜"-wide brown satin ribbon
Green and purple seed beads
1½"-wide antique button
2 small brass hinges

Small screwdriver (for hinges)
Large darning needle
Size 3 crewel embroidery needle
Beading needle
Masking tape
1" wooden dowel

Heavy Cardboard	Inside Fabric	Outer Fabric
INSIDE TOP, INSIDE BOTTOM, INSIDE SIDE	INSIDE SIDE + ¾"*	OUTSIDE SIDE
OUTSIDE TOP SIDE-cut 2	INSIDE BOTTOM + ¾"*	(FRONT and BACK)
INSIDE TOP SIDE-cut 2	INSIDE TOP + ¾"*	41" x 4¾"
OUTSIDE TOP-cut 2	INSIDE TOP SIDE + ¾"*	BASE + ¾"*
BASE-cut 2	-cut 2	OUTSIDE TOP
OUTSIDE SIDE (LEFT and RIGHT)-cut 4		17" x 10¾"
OUTSIDE SIDE (FRONT and BACK)-cut 4		

* See page 8.

Slip INSIDE TOP into OUTSIDE TOP. Glue together ¼" from outer edges all around. Glue ¼"-wide black cording into space between INSIDE TOP and OUTSIDE TOP at edges.

Glue black narrow trim to bottom edge of OUTSIDE TOP.

Hinge box top to box bottom with brass hinges, using small screwdriver. Cut ⅜"-wide brown satin ribbon in half. Glue 1-half to each inside side of box so top will not flip backwards. Glue antique button to center front edge of box top.

#	Stitch	Ribbon
1	JAPANESE RIBBON STITCH	Hunter green 7mm
2	KNOTTED LAZY DAISY	Burgundy 7mm
3	JAPANESE RIBBON STITCH	Olive green 7mm
4	FRENCH KNOTS	Burgundy textured 7mm
5	BULLION LAZY DAISY	Burgundy 2mm grosgrain
6	LAZY DAISY	Rust ¼-wide satin
7	STEM STITCH	Hunter green 4mm
8	STEM STITCH	Teal 4mm
9	BULLION LAZY DAISY	Burgundy 4mm
10	BULLION LAZY DAISY	Dk. purple 4mm
11	BULLION LAZY DAISY	Hunter green 4mm
12	BULLION LAZY DAISY	Teal 4mm
13	BULLION LAZY DAISY	Gold 4mm
14	BULLION LAZY DAISY	Red 4mm
15	FRENCH KNOT	Gold 4mm
16	TWISTED JAPANESE RIBBON STITCH	Burgundy 4mm
17	TWISTED JAPANESE RIBBON STITCH	Dk. purple 4mm
18	BEADING STITCH	Green and purple seed beads

Stitch Guide (See page 87.)

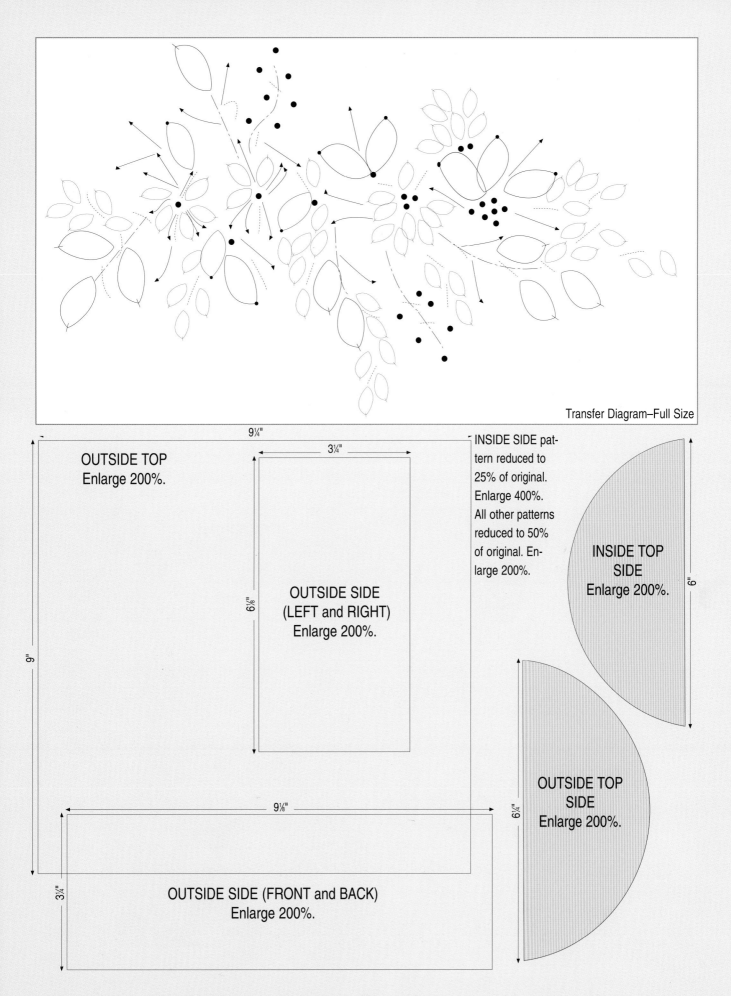

Transfer Diagram—Full Size

OUTSIDE TOP
Enlarge 200%.

9¼"

3¼"

OUTSIDE SIDE
(LEFT and RIGHT)
Enlarge 200%.

6⅞"

9"

INSIDE SIDE pat-
tern reduced to
25% of original.
Enlarge 400%.
All other patterns
reduced to 50%
of original. En-
large 200%.

INSIDE TOP
SIDE
Enlarge 200%.

6"

OUTSIDE TOP
SIDE
Enlarge 200%.

6¼"

9⅛"

3¼"

OUTSIDE SIDE (FRONT and BACK)
Enlarge 200%.

89

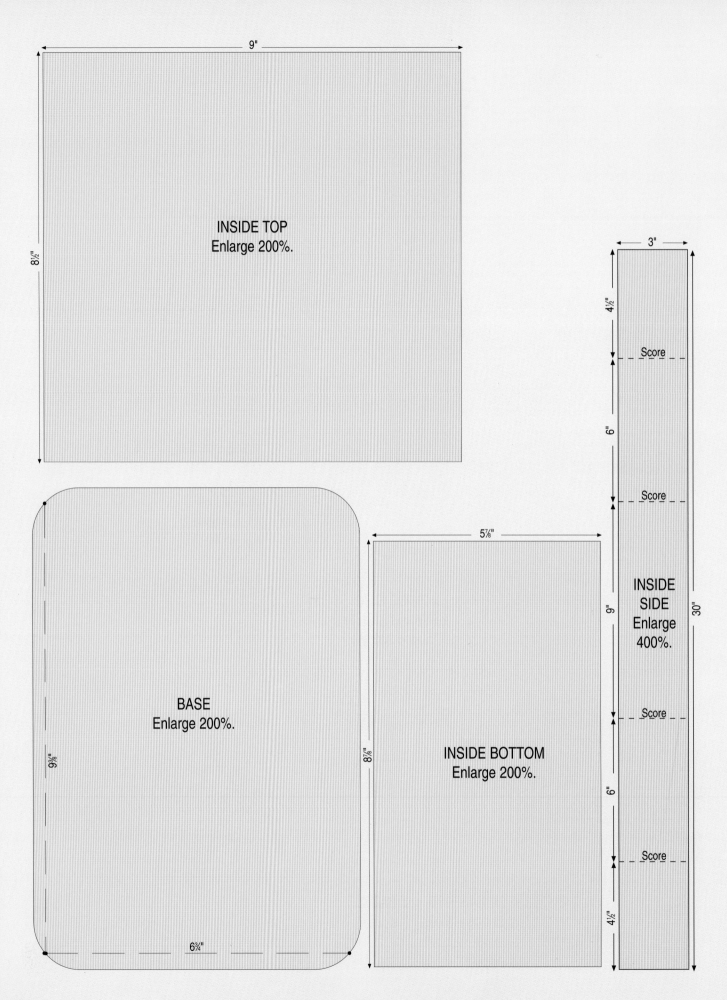

INSIDE TOP
Enlarge 200%.

9"

8½"

3"

4½"

Score

6"

Score

INSIDE
SIDE
Enlarge
400%.

30"

BASE
Enlarge 200%.

9⅜"

6¾"

5⅞"

9"

8⅞"

INSIDE BOTTOM
Enlarge 200%.

Score

6"

Score

4½"

• *Cut Cardboard and Fabric*

• *Cover Cardboard with Fabric and Shape*

Laminate INSIDE BOX SIDES A and B with inside fabric. Finish all 4 sides of each. Roll each with 1" dowel, right side up.

Follow instructions for *"Laminating Lid Strip"* of hidden-lid-strip-style boxes on page 13 for HIDDEN LID STRIPS A and B.

Laminate OUTSIDE BOX SIDES A and B with outer fabric. Place cardboard ¾" up from 1 long edge and centered between short edges. Finish all 4 sides of each. Roll with 1" dowel, wrong side up.

Laminate inside fabric to INSIDE LIDS A and B. Laminate outside fabric to LIDS, A and B. Laminate out-

side fabric to BASE B. Pad and wrap INSIDE BOTTOMS A and B with inside fabric.

• *Assemble Boxes*

Follow instructions for *"Assembling Box Bottom"* of hidden-lid-strip-style boxes on page 12. Note: OUTSIDE BOX SIDE stands ¾" taller than INSIDE BOX SIDE.

Follow instructions for *"Assembling Lid"* for hidden-lid-strip-style boxes on page 13. Glue wrong side of LID to wrong side of assembled lid, for boxes A and B.

• *Embellish Boxes*

Trim bottom sides of box A and B with 1½"-wide burgundy polka dot ribbon. Glue in place.

FLUTE ⅜"-wide khaki green grosgrain ribbon while gluing to bottom edge of box B. Glue BASE B to bottom of box B.

KNIFE-PLEAT 1"-wide olive green wired ribbon while gluing to bottom of box A. Glue bottom of box A to LID of box B.

• *Embellish Dress Form*

Embellish small dress form as desired. Wrap dress form's base with scraps of fabric. Cover raw edge with trim. FLUTE ⅜"-wide khaki green grosgrain ribbon while gluing to underside edge of base. Glue dress form base to box LID A. Drape back of dress form with large bows as desired.

Tools and Materials
Heavy cardboard–11" x 22"
Lightweight cardboard–14" x 18"
Outer fabric (khaki green antique velvet)–¼ yd.
Inside fabric (aqua patterned satin)–¼ yd.
Quilt batting–5" x 10"
1⅛ yd. of 1½"-wide burgundy polka dot ribbon
2 yds. of ⅜"-wide khaki green grosgrain ribbon
30" of 1"-wide wired olive green ribbon
Small purchased dress form (Note: Base of dress form must be a little smaller than LID A.)
Embellishments for dress form– scraps of unusual fabrics and trims, ribbons and beads
1" wooden dowel

Heavy Cardboard	Light Cardboard	Inside Fabric	Outer Fabric

LID A
INSIDE BOTTOM and
  INSIDE LID A-cut 2
LID and BASE B-cut 2
INSIDE BOTTOM and
  INSIDE LID B-cut 2
	INSIDE BOX SIDE A
	OUTSIDE BOX SIDE A
	LID STRIP A
	INSIDE BOX SIDE B
	OUTSIDE BOX SIDE B
	LID STRIP B
		INSIDE BOX SIDE A + ½"*
		LID STRIP A 2½" x 13½"
		INSIDE BOTTOM and
		  INSIDE LID A + ½"*-cut 2
		INSIDE BOX SIDE B + ½"*
		LID STRIP B 2½" x 16½"
		INSIDE BOTTOM and
		  INSIDE LID B + ¾"*-cut 2
			OUTSIDE BOX SIDE
			  A 3¾" x 14"
			LID A + ½"*
			OUTSIDE BOX SIDE
			  B 5" x 17½"
			BASE B +½"*
			LID and BASE B
			  + ¾"*

* See page 8.

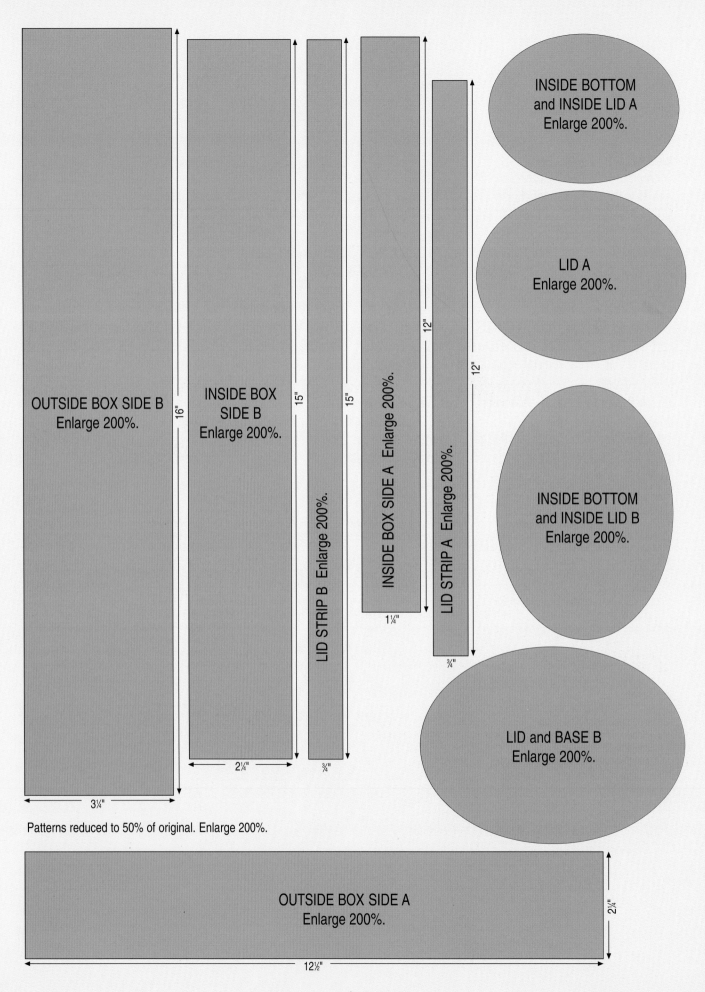

OUTSIDE BOX SIDE B
Enlarge 200%.

16"

3¼"

INSIDE BOX
SIDE B
Enlarge 200%.

15"

2¼"

LID STRIP B Enlarge 200%.

15"

¾"

INSIDE BOX SIDE A Enlarge 200%.

12"

1¼"

LID STRIP A Enlarge 200%.

12"

¾"

INSIDE BOTTOM
and INSIDE LID A
Enlarge 200%.

LID A
Enlarge 200%.

INSIDE BOTTOM
and INSIDE LID B
Enlarge 200%.

LID and BASE B
Enlarge 200%.

Patterns reduced to 50% of original. Enlarge 200%.

OUTSIDE BOX SIDE A
Enlarge 200%.

2¼"

12½"

• **Cut Cardboard and Fabric, Score**

For each DRAWER piece, mark location of button and puncture cardboard at mark with large needle or awl. For CLOTHES CLOSET SECTION, mark location of cording insert and puncture cardboard at mark with large needle or awl.

• **Cover Cardboard with Fabric, Shape and Assemble Inside Box Structure**

Laminate unscored side of 4 DRAWER SHELVINGS with drawer shelving fabric. Finish 2 long edges and 1 short edge. Fold at each score and emphasize scores. Join short edges of each cardboard piece by overlapping finished short edge to tab edge and butting cardboard edges up to each other. Glue tab in place. Squarely glue 3 of assembled DRAWER SHELVING pieces together at a matching 6"-long side. Remaining DRAWER SHELVING is for opposite side of steamer.

Laminate unscored side of MIDDLE SHELVING, TOP SHELVING, and CLOTHES CLOSET SECTION with inside fabric. Finish 2 long edges and 1 short edge. Fold at each score and emphasize scores. Roll each 7½" section of TOP SHELVING and CLOTHES CLOSET SECTION with 1" dowel, fabric side up. Join short edges of each cardboard piece by overlapping finished short edges to tab edge. Glue tabs in place.

Squarely glue MIDDLE SHELVING to top of assembled drawer shelving unit at matching 6"-long side. Squarely glue TOP SHELVING to top of MIDDLE SHELVING at 6"-long side. This is the completed inside left steamer unit.

Squarely glue CLOTHES CLOSET SECTION to remaining DRAWER SHELVING at matching 6"-long side. Insert narrow cording through holes at center top of CLOTHES CLOSET SECTION. Glue edges of cording to wrong side. Let cording drape about ½" at inside center front. This is the completed inside right steamer unit.

Laminate each INSIDE BACK with inside fabric. Glue an INSIDE BACK to inside left steamer unit and inside right steamer unit. Glue ⅝"-wide lt. green iridescent ribbon to wrong side of front edge of inside right steamer unit at marks.

• **Cover Cardboard with Fabric, Shape and Assemble Outside Box Structure**

Roll each OUTSIDE BOX SIDE C with 1" dowel to shape steamer top. Glue 2 layers of cardboard together for OUTSIDE BOX SIDE sections A, B, and C. There is a total of 4 A sections, 4 B sections and 2 C sections. Lay outer fabric wrong side up on work surface. Laminate 1 section A, ¾" from right edge of strip and centered. Mark a ⅛" space on left side of first section A. Place and laminate 1 section B at mark, so long edges are lined up. Mark a ⅛" space on left side of first section B. Place and laminate 1 section C at mark, so long edges are lined up. (Cardboard and fabric will begin to get awkward because section C curves). Mark ⅛" space on left side of section C. Place and laminate a second section B at mark, lining up long edges. Wrap 2 short edges and 1 long edge of fabric onto cardboard pieces. Repeat entire process again for second OUTSIDE BOX SIDE.

Beginning at center bottom, glue OUTSIDE BOX SIDE to inside left steamer unit, wrong sides together. Line back edge of inside left steamer unit up to back, unwrapped edge of

---

Heavy Cardboard	Inside Fabric	Outer Fabric
DRAWER SHELVING-cut 4 MIDDLE SHELVING TOP SHELVING CLOTHES CLOSET SECTION INSIDE BACK-cut 2 OUTSIDE BOX SIDE A (BOTTOM)-cut 8 OUTSIDE BOX SIDE B (SIDES)-cut 8 OUTSIDE BOX SIDE C (CURVED TOPS)-cut 4 OUTSIDE BOX BASE-cut 2 BACK-cut 2 DRAWER INSIDE BOTTOM AND BASE-cut 8 DRAWER FRONT STABILIZER-cut 4 DRAWER-cut 4	OUTSIDE BOX SIDE 4¾" x 40¼"-cut 2 OUTSIDE BOX BASE + ¾"*-cut 2 BACK + ¾"*-cut 2 **Drawer Fabric** DRAWER 18½" x 4½"-cut 4 DRAWER INSIDE BOTTOM + ½"-cut 4 DRAWER BASE + ½"*-cut 4 DRAWER FRONT STABILIZER + ½"*-cut 4	MIDDLE SHELVING 18½" x 4" TOP SHELVING 22" x 4" CLOTHES CLOSET SECTION 35½" x 4" INSIDE BACK + ¾"*-cut 2 **Drawer Shelving Fabric** 4 pieces 17½" x 4" 2 pieces 5⅞" x 4"

* See page 8.

OUTSIDE BOX SIDE. Glue 1 section at a time and use a lot of glue. Pull OUTSIDE BOX SIDE very tight for a snug fit. Wrap and glue unwrapped edge of OUTSIDE BOX SIDE onto wrong side of INSIDE BACK.

Laminate half of each DRAWER SHELVING BOTTOM with drawer shelving fabric to inside of bottom shelf. Wrap liner to underside of OUTSIDE BOX SIDE.

Laminate each BACK with outer fabric. Glue each BACK to INSIDE BACK, wrong sides together. Work quickly and use a lot of glue.

Laminate each OUTSIDE BOX BASE with outer fabric. Glue each BASE to bottom of steamer.

• Cover Cardboard with Fabric, Shape and Assemble Drawers

Laminate each DRAWER INSIDE BOTTOM, DRAWER FRONT STABILIZER, and BASE with drawer fabric. Finish all 4 sides.

Laminate each unscored side of DRAWER with drawer fabric. Finish 2 long edges and 1 short edge. Place fabric side up on work surface. Fold at each score and emphasize scores.

Overlap finished edge to tab edge, and butt cardboard edges up to each other. Glue tab in place.

Working upside down, slip INSIDE BOTTOM into each DRAWER 1/16" down from DRAWER'S edge. Glue in place. Glue a BASE to underside of each DRAWER. Glue a DRAWER FRONT STABILIZER to each inside front of DRAWER. Puncture through FRONT STABILIZER. Attach button or drawer pull to drawer front.

Attach back hinges and front clasp to steamer.

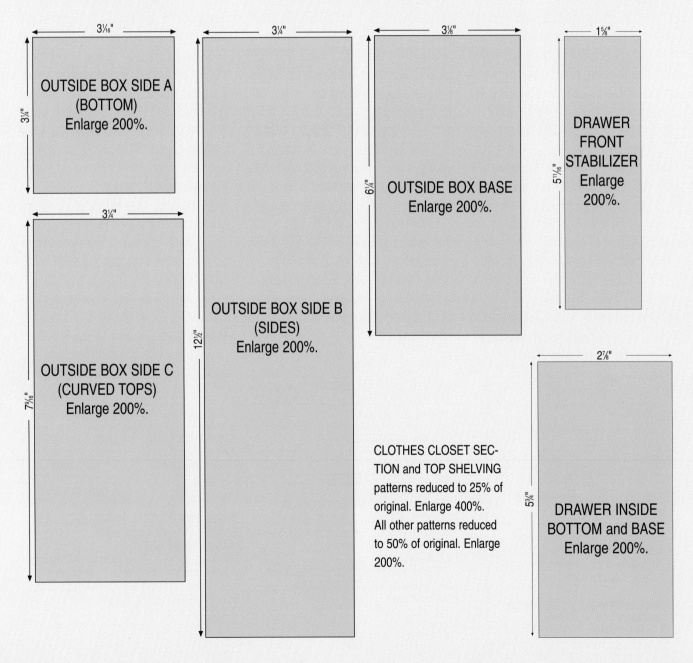

OUTSIDE BOX SIDE A (BOTTOM) Enlarge 200%. 3 1/16" × 3 1/4"

OUTSIDE BOX SIDE B (SIDES) Enlarge 200%. 3 1/4" × 12 1/2"

OUTSIDE BOX SIDE C (CURVED TOPS) Enlarge 200%. 3 1/4" × 7 9/16"

OUTSIDE BOX BASE Enlarge 200%. 3 1/8" × 6 1/4"

DRAWER FRONT STABILIZER Enlarge 200%. 1 5/8" × 5 11/16"

DRAWER INSIDE BOTTOM and BASE Enlarge 200%. 2 7/8" × 5 3/4"

CLOTHES CLOSET SECTION and TOP SHELVING patterns reduced to 25% of original. Enlarge 400%. All other patterns reduced to 50% of original. Enlarge 200%.

98

INSIDE BACK
Enlarge 200%

12½"

14⅜"

6⅛"

BACK
Enlarge 200%

12⅝"

14½"

6¼"

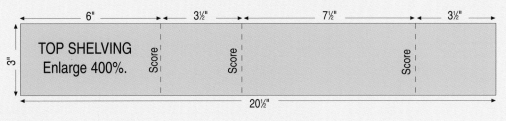

6"   3½"   7½"   3½"

TOP SHELVING
Enlarge 400%.

3"

Score   Score   Score

20½"

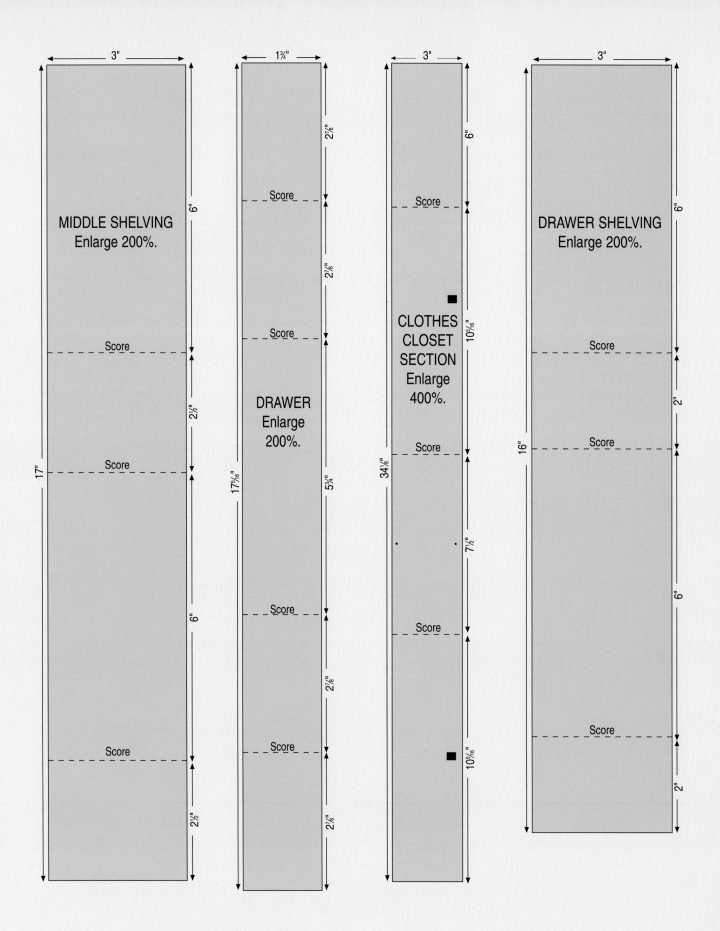

MIDDLE SHELVING
Enlarge 200%.

3"

6"

Score

2½"

Score

6"

17"

Score

2½"

DRAWER
Enlarge 200%.

1¾"

2⅞"

Score

2⅞"

Score

17⁵⁄₁₆"

5¾"

Score

2⅞"

Score

2⅞"

CLOTHES
CLOSET
SECTION
Enlarge 400%.

3"

6"

Score

10⁵⁄₁₆"

34⅛"

Score

7½"

Score

10⁵⁄₁₆"

DRAWER SHELVING
Enlarge 200%.

3"

6"

Score

2"

Score

16"

6"

Score

2"

• Cut Cardboard and Fabric, Score

• Cover Cardboard with Fabric and Shape

Laminate BASE and MIDDLE LID with outer fabric. Trim as much bulk as possible. Laminate fabric onto opposite side of MIDDLE LID as shown on pattern.

Laminate mountain-scored side of BOX SIDE with outer fabric. Finish 2 long edges and 1 short edge. Place right side up on work surface. Fold at each valley score, and emphasize scores. Place wrong side up on work surface. Fold at each mountain score, and emphasize scores. Roll entire BOX SIDE, wrong side up, with 1" dowel for initial shaping. Roll handle, bottom half of spout, and entire lid area with ½" dowel. Turn right side up, and roll top of spout with ¼" dowel. Pinch knob- and lid-indented areas. Stand BOX SIDE up, and mold with fingers for any additional shaping to match INSIDE BOTTOM.

Glue 3 INSIDE LIDS together. Laminate combined INSIDE LID with inside fabric. INSIDE BOTTOM is not wrapped with fabric. Embroider LID fabric before pad and wrap process.

• Assemble Box Bottom

Follow instructions for *"Assembling Box Bottom"* of hinge-lid-style boxes on page 12. Remember this box does not have a ribbon hinge!

Follow instructions for *"Lining Strips"* of hinge-lid-style boxes on page 12. Glue INSIDE BOTTOM fabric onto LINING STRIP

Turn box upside down. FLUTE ¼"-wide dk. green velvet ribbon while gluing onto underside of box. Glue wrong side of BASE to bottom of box.

Glue wrong side of INSIDE LID to right side of MIDDLE LID.

• Embellish and Finish Box

Following stitch guide and chart on page 104, embroider LID fabric. Assemble large flowers (1–3). Place flowers and invisibly stitch onto LID, following stitch guide. Continue embroidering LID.

Pad LID with 1 layer of batting, and wrap with embroidered fabric. FLUTE ¼"-wide dk. green velvet ribbon while gluing to underside edge of LID. Glue wrong side of LID to wrong side MIDDLE LID.

Tools and Materials
Heavy cardboard–12" x 18"
Lightweight cardboard–3" x 18"
Outer fabric (green velvet)–12" x 22"
Inside fabric (bright yellow velvet)– 12" x 15"
Lid fabric (green satin)–6" x 8"
Quilt batting–5" x 14"
2 yds. of ¼"-wide dk. green velvet ribbon
15" of 1"-wide yellow ombré wired ribbon; matching thread
11" of 1"-wide pink ombré wired ribbon; matching thread
15" of 1"-wide orange ombré wired ribbon; matching thread
18" of dk. green iridescent 7mm ribbon
18" each of dk. blue, lt green, and olive green 7mm ribbon
54" of yellow 7mm ribbon
18" of orange, gold, white, blue green and red 4mm ribbon
72" of lt. green 4mm ribbon
54" each of dk. and lt. olive green 4mm ribbon
36" each of purple and red/ violet 4mm ribbon
Hand sewing needle
Beading needle
Size 3 crewel embroidery needle
Size 20 chenille needle
1", ½" and ¼" wooden dowels

Heavy Cardboard	Light Cardboard	Inside Fabric	Outer Fabric
INSIDE BOTTOM LID INSIDE LID–cut 3 BASE and MIDDLE cut 2	BOX SIDE LINING STRIP	INSIDE BOTTOM pattern INSIDE LID (facing left) + ¾"*	BOX SIDE + ½"* BASE (facing left) + ½"* MIDDLE LID (facing left) + ½"* **Lid Fabric** LID

* See page 8.

#	*Stitch*	*Ribbon*
1	Marigold	Yellow ombré 1" wired ribbon
2	Azalea	Pink ombré 1" wired ribbon
3	Dwarf Dahlia	Orange ombré 1" wired ribbon
4	Folded Leaf	Dk. green iridescent 7mm ribbon
5	Squared Leaf	Dk. green iridescent 7mm ribbon
6	Bullion Lazy Daisy	Olive green 7mm ribbon
7	Japanese Ribbon Stitch	Lt. green 7mm ribbon
8	Bullion Lazy Daisy	Yellow 7mm ribbon
9	Japanese Ribbon Stitch	Orange 4mm ribbon
10	French Knot	Gold 4mm ribbon
11	Japanese Ribbon Stitch	White 4mm ribbon
12	French Knot	Yellow 7mm ribbon
13	Twisted Japanese Ribbon Stitch	Blue green 4mm ribbon
14	French Knot	Dk. blue 7mm ribbon
15	Lazy Daisy	Lt. green 4mm ribbon
16	French Knot	Purple 4mm ribbon
17	French Knot	Red/violet 4mm ribbon
18	Bullion Lazy Daisy	Red 4mm ribbon
19	Lazy Daisy	Dk. olive green 4mm ribbon
20	Lazy Daisy	Lt. olive green 4mm ribbon
21	Japanese Ribbon Stitch	Lt. green 4mm ribbon

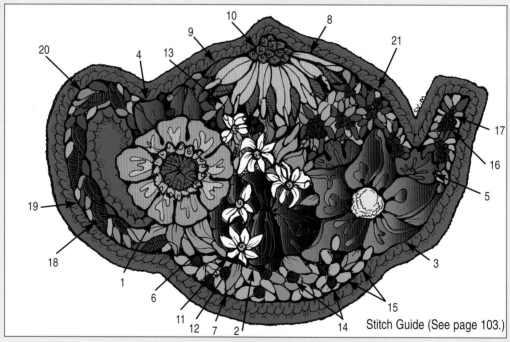

Stitch Guide (See page 103.)

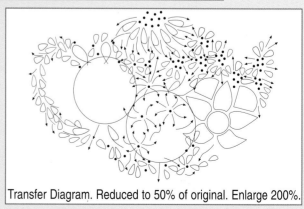

Transfer Diagram. Reduced to 50% of original. Enlarge 200%.

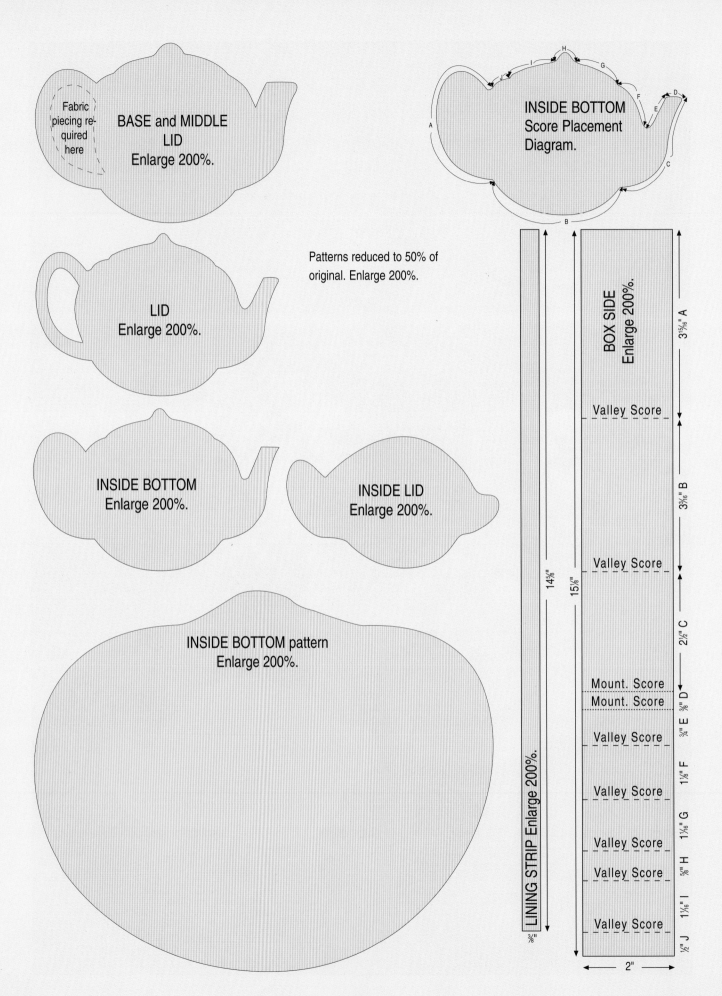

BASE and MIDDLE
LID
Enlarge 200%.

Fabric piecing required here

INSIDE BOTTOM
Score Placement
Diagram.

LID
Enlarge 200%.

Patterns reduced to 50% of
original. Enlarge 200%.

INSIDE BOTTOM
Enlarge 200%.

INSIDE LID
Enlarge 200%.

INSIDE BOTTOM pattern
Enlarge 200%.

LINING STRIP Enlarge 200%.

⅜"

14⅝"

15⅛"

BOX SIDE
Enlarge 200%.

3¹⁵⁄₁₆" A

Valley Score

3³⁄₁₆" B

Valley Score

2½" C

Mount. Score

Mount. Score ⅜" D

¾" E

Valley Score

1⅛" F

Valley Score

1¹⁄₁₆" G

Valley Score

⅝" H

Valley Score

1¹⁄₁₆" I

Valley Score

½" J

2"

• *Cut Cardboard and Fabric, Score*

• *Cover Inner Structure with Fabric and Assemble*

Laminate DRESSER INNER STRUCTURE SHELVES with outer fabric. Cut slash lines through fabric where located on cardboard. Edge with slash lines is front edge of box.

Laminate DRESSER INNER STRUCTURE SIDES with outer fabric, 1 left facing and 1 right facing. Trim excess fabric flush to cardboard's edge. Cut slash lines through fabric where located on cardboard. Fold score mark on SIDES at bottom and top edge outward from fabric-covered side of cardboard, and emphasize scores.

Slip 1 SHELF, fabric side up, into bottom slash lines on each SIDE. Fold scored tab edge outward, then glue tab to underside of bottom SHELF at slash line. Slip 1 SHELF, fabric side up, into second from bottom slash lines on each SIDE. Hold in place, while gluing left slash line and right slash line. (Glue on side without fabric.) Slip 1 SHELF, fabric side up, into third from bottom slash

lines on each SIDE. Glue in place in same manner. Slip top SHELF, fabric side down, into top slash line on each SIDE. Fold scored top tab edge outward, then glue tab to underside of top SHELF at slash line.

Roll BOX SIDE STRUCTURE LINING with 1" dowel. Fold front edge tabs inward to curving cardboard.

Beginning at left front edge of oval drawer structure, fold and glue tab edge of BOX SIDE STRUCTURE LINING to inside front edge of left shelving side. Pull firmly while wrapping LINING around oval structure so right tab edge can be glued to inside front edge of right shelving side. Tape top and bottom edge of LINING to edge of top and bottom shelves.

Cover front edges of BOX SIDE STRUCTURE LINING at shelves with laminated inside fabric strips. Slash fabric strips where necessary to wrap to inside sides of shelving.

• *Laminate and Assemble Tray*

Laminate TOP TRAY with inside fabric. Glue and place TRAY STRIP ¼" up from 1 long edge of fabric and centered between short edges. Fol-

low instructions for *"Laminating Lid Strip"* of hidden-lid-strip-style boxes on page 13.

Join short edges of TRAY STRIP by overlapping finished short edge to tab edge and butting cardboard edges up to each other. Glue tab in place. Slip TOP TRAY, wrong side up, into TRAY STRIP at extended fabric edge, so TRAY STRIP joint is at a center side. Snugly glue extended fabric over onto wrong side of TOP TRAY, pulling fabric as tight as possible. Continue to glue extended fabric of TRAY STRIP completely onto TOP TRAY. Thoroughly flatten glue. Glue underside of assembled TRAY to top of shelving structure.

• *Laminate and Assemble Outside Box Side*

Laminate OUTSIDE BOX SIDE with outer fabric. Finish all 4 edges. Roll wrong side up with 1" dowel. Beginning at left front edge of assembled shelving structure, glue side edge of OUTSIDE BOX SIDE to structure, ⅛" away from left front edge. Snugly pull OUTSIDE BOX SIDE around structure. Glue remain-

---

Tools and Materials

Heavy cardboard–20" x 30"
Lightweight cardboard–20" x 30"
Outer fabric (pansy cotton print)–1 yd.
Inside fabric (purple on purple cotton print)–½ yd.
Quilt batting–8" x 6"

3 small buttons or drawer pulls
Thread (if using buttons)

Large needle (able to stitch through cardboard)
Masking tape
1" wooden dowel

Heavy Cardboard	Light Cardboard	Inside Fabric	Outer Fabric
TOP TRAY	OUTSIDE BOX SIDE	INSIDE LID + ½"*	OUTSIDE BOX SIDE
DRESSER INNER	BOX SIDE STRUCTURE	TOP TRAY + ½"*	+ ½"*
STRUCTURE SIDE	LINING	BOX SIDE STRUCTURE	LID STRIP 3" x 24½"
-cut 2	LID STRIP	LINING-6¼" x 2"-cut 2	TRAY STRIP
BASE, INSIDE LID	TRAY STRIP	DRAWER SIDE-4½" x	2¾" x 23¼"
and LID-cut 3	DRAWER SIDE-cut 3	18¾"-cut 3	BASE and LID + ¾"-
DRAWER BASE-cut 3	DRAWER FRONT-cut 3		cut 2
INSIDE DRAWER			DRAWER FRONT
BOTTOM- cut 3			4" x 7½"-cut 3
DRESSER INNER			DRAWER BASE and
STRUCTURE			INSIDE DRAWER
SHELVES-cut 4			BOTTOM + ½"-cut 3
			DRESSER INNER
			STRUCTURE
			SIDE + ½"*-cut 2
			DRAWER FRONT
			DRAWER BASE and
			INSIDE DRAWER
			BOTTOM + ½"*-cut 3
			DRESSER INNER
			STRUCTURE
			SHELF + ½"*-cut 4

* See page 8.

ing front edge to ⅛" away from right front edge. Invisibly slip hot glue in between TRAY STRIP and top edge of OUTSIDE BOX SIDE; glue edges together. Repeat with bottom edge.

Laminate BASE with outer fabric. Glue wrong side of BASE to underside of oval dresser.

• *Laminate and Assemble Lid*

Laminate INSIDE LID with inside fabric. Glue and place LID STRIP ¼" up from 1 long edge of fabric and centered between short edges. Follow instructions for *"Laminating Lid Strip"* of hidden-lid-strip-style boxes on page 13.

Join short edges of LID STRIP by overlapping finished short edge to tab edge and butting cardboard edges up to each other. Glue tab in place. Follow instructions for *"Assembling Lid"* of hidden-lid-strip-style boxes on page 13.

Pad LID with batting, then wrap with outer fabric. Glue wrong side of padded LID to top of assembled LID.

• *Laminate and Assemble Drawers*

Laminate each INSIDE DRAWER BOTTOM, and DRAWER BASE with inside fabric. Laminate DRAWER FRONT with outer fabric.

Laminate unscored side of each DRAWER SIDE with inside fabric, ¼" up from 1 long edge and centered between short edges of fabric. Trim off ¼" excess fabric from bottom edge of cardboard. Place DRAWER SIDE wrong side up on work surface. Paint ½" of 1 short edge of fabric with glue. Wrap short edge over on itself at cardboard's edge. Remaining short edge will be a fabric tab. Paint opposite side of DRAWER SIDE with glue. Wrap fabric onto glued cardboard

and smooth completely. DRAWER SIDE is now completely covered with fabric with ½" of fabric extending past cardboard's edge. Roll front section of DRAWER SIDE with 1" dowel, trimmed edge side up. Continue to assemble as for top tray. Repeat for all 3 drawers.

Glue DRAWER BASE to each assembled drawer.

Mark each DRAWER FRONT for button placement. Puncture cardboard at marks with needle. Lightly roll wrong side up with 1" dowel. Center and glue each DRAWER FRONT to curved edge of assembled drawer.

Stitch button in place for a drawer pull, through 2 layers of cardboard, using punctured DRAWER FRONT as placement guide.

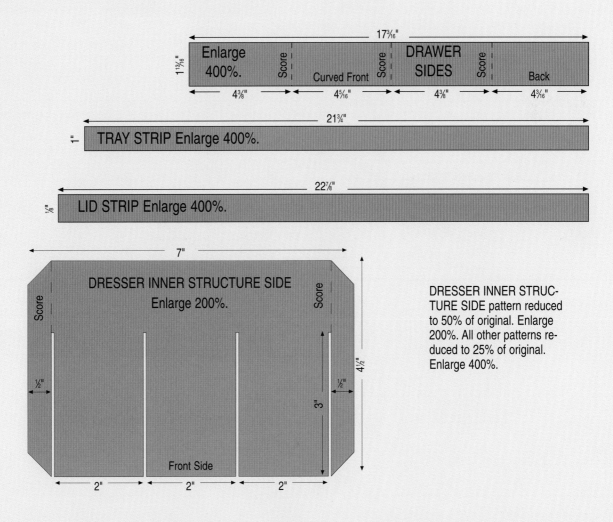

DRESSER INNER STRUCTURE SIDE pattern reduced to 50% of original. Enlarge 200%. All other patterns reduced to 25% of original. Enlarge 400%.

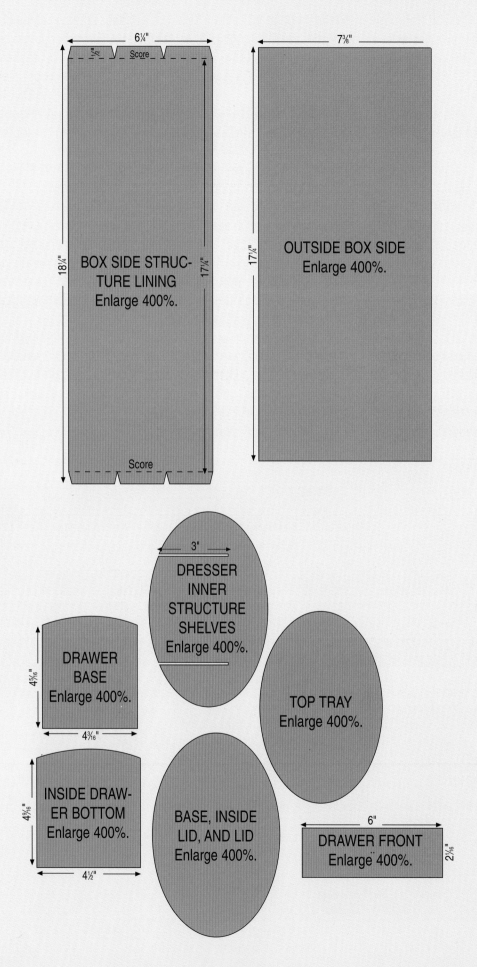

6¼"

½"

Score

18¼"

17¼"

BOX SIDE STRUC-
TURE LINING
Enlarge 400%.

Score

7⅜"

17¼"

OUTSIDE BOX SIDE
Enlarge 400%.

3"

DRESSER
INNER
STRUCTURE
SHELVES
Enlarge 400%.

DRAWER
BASE
Enlarge 400%.

4⁵⁄₁₆"

4³⁄₁₆"

TOP TRAY
Enlarge 400%.

INSIDE DRAW-
ER BOTTOM
Enlarge 400%.

4⁵⁄₁₆"

4½"

BASE, INSIDE
LID, AND LID
Enlarge 400%.

6"

DRAWER FRONT
Enlarge 400%.

2¹⁄₁₆"

French Curve

- ### Cut Cardboard and Fabric, Score

- ### Cover Cardboard with Fabric and Shape

Laminate unscored side of INSIDE BOX SIDE with inside fabric. Finish 2 long edges and 1 short edge. Place right side up on work surface. Fold at each score mark and emphasize scores. Carefully roll with 1" dowel right side up, beginning at outer short edge. Roll centers of 5 wide sections with ½" dowel for extra shaping. Place wrong side up on work surface. Roll in between each ¾" section with ¼" dowel. Roll right next to these sections, on either side, with ½" dowel for extra shaping. Stand box side up and place around INSIDE BOTTOM. Mold INSIDE BOX SIDE with fingers to further match INSIDE BOTTOM.

Follow instructions for "Laminating Lid Strip" of hidden-lid-strip-style boxes on page 13. Laminate unscored side of HIDDEN LID STRIP with inside fabric. Scored side of cardboard will be the outside of HIDDEN LID STRIP. Place unscored side up on work surface and shape like INSIDE BOX SIDE.

Laminate scored side of OUTSIDE BOX SIDE with outside fabric. Place ¾" up from 1 long edge and centered between short edges. Finish all 4 edges. Place wrong side up on work surface and shape like INSIDE BOX SIDE.

Laminate INSIDE LID and IN BETWEEN LID with inside fabric. Laminate BASE and MIDDLE LID with outer fabric. Pad and wrap INSIDE BOTTOM with inside fabric.

Embroider LID fabric before pad and wrap process.

- ### Assemble Box Bottom

Follow instructions for "Assembling Box Bottom" of hidden-lid-strip-style boxes on page 12. Glue OUTSIDE BOX SIDE to INSIDE BOX SIDE, matching seamed INSIDE BOX SIDE to 4⅜" section of OUTSIDE BOX SIDE. Work 2" to 3" at a time, matching all scores. Overlap finished edges at center back, and glue in place. Emphasize shape with fingers.

Glue wrong side of BASE to bottom of box.

- ### Assemble Lid

Follow instructions for "Assembling Lid" for hidden-lid-strip-style boxes on page 13. Match points of INSIDE LID with scores. Center and glue right side of MIDDLE LID to wrong side of assembled lid.

- ### Embellish Box

Turn IN BETWEEN LID upside down. FLUTE ¼"-wide burgundy velvet ribbon while gluing onto underside of IN BETWEEN LID. Glue wrong side of IN BETWEEN LID to wrong side of MIDDLE LID. Glue 1½"-wide chartreuse velvet ribbon to bottom side of box. Cover overlap at center back with flat bow. Glue ¼"-wide dk. green cording to bottom edge of box.

Following stitch guide and chart on page 114, embroider LID fabric.

Pad and wrap embroidered fabric to LID. Glue wrong side of LID to wrong side of IN BETWEEN LID.

Tools and Materials

Heavy cardboard–30" x 8"
Lightweight cardboard–22" x 10"
Outer fabric (burgundy moiré)–¼ yd.
Lid fabric (ivory satin, lace overlay)–9" x 7"
Inside fabric (chartreuse velvet)–¼ yd.
Quilt batting–7" x 18"

1¼ yd. of ¼"-wide burgundy velvet ribbon
30" of 1½"-wide chartreuse velvet ribbon
20" of ¼"-wide dark green cording
1 yd. each of wine, burgundy, hot pink, olive green, blue green, green and teal 4mm ribbon
1 yd. of dk. green 7mm ribbon
1 yd. each of lilac, purple, and pink silk floss
1 yd. each of dk. green, burgundy, and dk. rose embroidery floss
½ yd. of olive green corded floss
Olive, burgundy and strawberry seed beads
35 lt. rose bugle beads

Size 3 crewel embroidery needle
Size 20 chenille needle
Beading needle
1", ½" and ¼" wooden dowels

Heavy Cardboard	Light Cardboard	Inside Fabric	Outer Fabric
INSIDE BOTTOM, INSIDE LID, LID–cut 3 BASE and MIDDLE LID –cut 2	IN BETWEEN LID INSIDE BOX SIDE HIDDEN LID STRIP OUTSIDE BOX SIDE	INSIDE BOTTOM and INSIDE LID + ¾"* –cut 2 IN BETWEEN LID + ½"* INSIDE BOX SIDE + ¾"* HIDDEN LID STRIP 2½" x 18½"	BASE and MIDDLE LID + ½"*–cut 2 OUTSIDE BOX SIDE 6" x 20½" **Lid Fabric** LID + ¾"*

* See page 8.

#	Stitch	Ribbon and Floss
1	COUCHING STITCH	3 strands of dk. green floss
2	COUCHING STITCH	Olive green corded floss
3	BULLION LAZY DAISY	Wine 4mm ribbon
4	JAPANESE RIBBON STITCH	Wine 4mm ribbon
5	TWISTED JAPANESE RIBBON STITCH	Hot pink 4mm ribbon
6	JAPANESE RIBBON STITCH	Burgundy 4 mm ribbon
7	BULLION ROSE	Lilac silk floss
8	BULLION ROSE	Purple silk floss
9	BULLION ROSE	Pink silk floss
10	STRAIGHT STITCH	6 strands of burgundy floss
11	STRAIGHT STITCH	6 strands of dk. rose floss
12	LAZY DAISY	Dk. green 7mm ribbon
13	LAZY DAISY	Blue green 4mm ribbon
14	LAZY DAISY	Olive green 4mm ribbon
15	JAPANESE RIBBON STITCH	Green 4mm ribbon
16	JAPANESE RIBBON STITCH	Teal 4mm ribbon
17	BEADING STITCH	Lt. rose bugle beads
18	BEADING STITCH	Olive, burgundy and strawberry seed beads

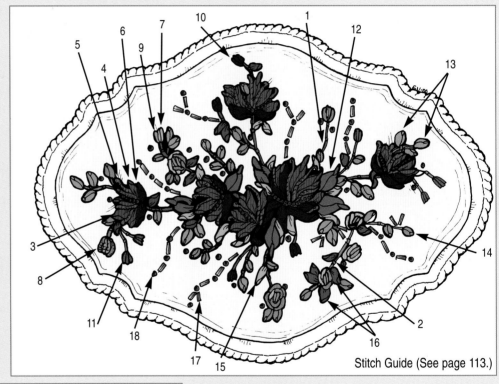

Stitch Guide (See page 113.)

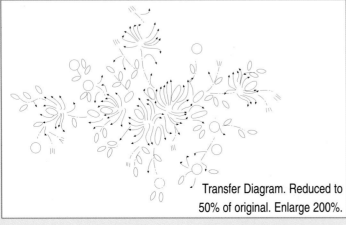

Transfer Diagram. Reduced to
50% of original. Enlarge 200%.

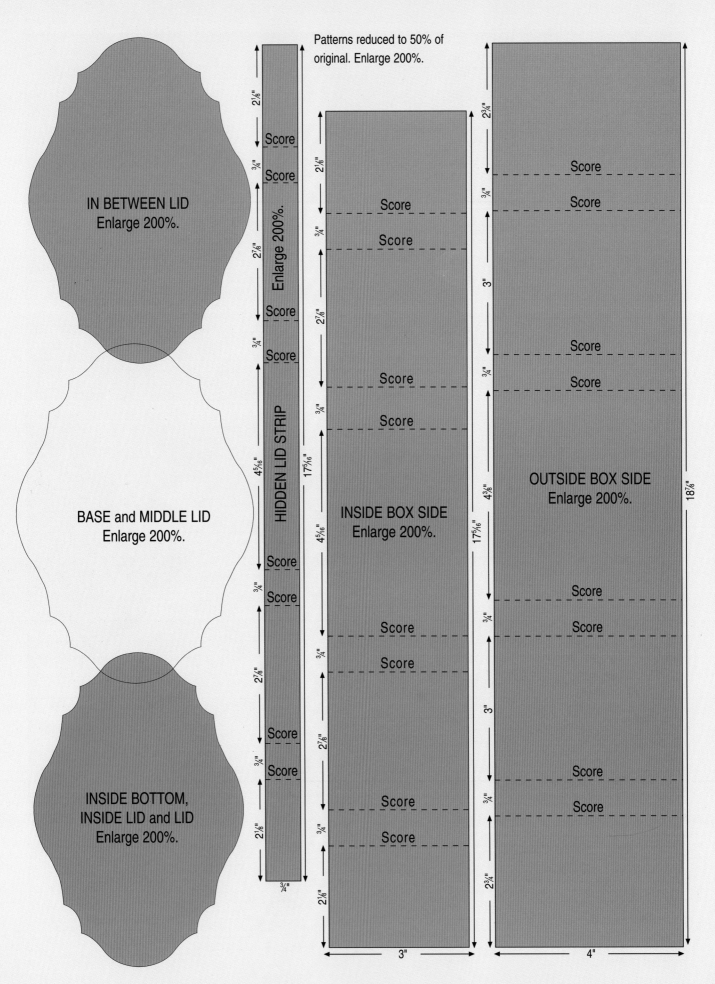

IN BETWEEN LID
Enlarge 200%.

BASE and MIDDLE LID
Enlarge 200%.

INSIDE BOTTOM,
INSIDE LID and LID
Enlarge 200%.

HIDDEN LID STRIP

Enlarge 200%.

2⅛"

Score

Score

¾"

2⅞"

Score

Score

4⁵⁄₁₆"

Score

Score

2⅞"

Score

Score

2⅛"

¾"

INSIDE BOX SIDE
Enlarge 200%.

2⅛"

Score

Score

¾"

2⅞"

Score

Score

¾"

4⁵⁄₁₆"

17⁵⁄₁₆"

Score

Score

¾"

2⅞"

Score

Score

¾"

2⅛"

3"

Patterns reduced to 50% of
original. Enlarge 200%.

OUTSIDE BOX SIDE
Enlarge 200%.

2¾"

Score

Score

¾"

3"

Score

Score

¾"

4⅜"

17⁵⁄₁₆"

18⅞"

Score

Score

¾"

3"

Score

Score

¾"

2¾"

4"

116

Autumn Leaf

• Cut Cardboard and Fabric, Score

• Cover Outside Box Side with Fabric and Shape

Cut brown fabric scraps in various shapes. Laminate to mountain-scored side of OUTSIDE BOX SIDE. Piece as desired, crazy-quilt style, butting raw edges of fabrics up to each other. Raw edges are not turned under. Allow brown fabric scraps, to extend 1" beyond cardboard. Completely smooth brown fabric scraps and make sure they are entirely adhered to all edges of cardboard. Finish all 4 sides. Cover raw edges with trims, and carefully glue in place.

Place OUTSIDE BOX SIDE right side up on work surface. Fold at each valley score mark and emphasize scores. Place right side down on work surface. Fold at each mountain score and emphasize scores. Carefully roll entire OUTSIDE BOX SIDE with 1" dowel. At each valley score, roll leaf points. Place right side up on

work surface. At each mountain score, roll with ½" dowel to add extra shape to leaf points.

• Cover Lid with Fabric

Lay iron-on fusing on top of LID fabric. Place pieces of solid outer fabric crazy-quilt style on top of fusing material, butting raw edges together. When desired look is achieved, iron pieces in place. Trim edges flush with leaf shape. Cover raw edges with assorted trims.

• Cover Remaining Cardboard with Fabric and Shape

Laminate BASE and MIDDLE LID with solid outer fabric. Pad INSIDE BOTTOM and INSIDE LID with 1 layer of batting, then wrap with inside fabric.

Laminate valley-scored side of INSIDE BOX SIDE with inside fabric. Leave 1 short edge unfinished. Shape like OUTSIDE BOX SIDE, working with INSIDE BOX SIDE wrong side up.

• Assemble Box Bottom

Follow instructions for "Assembling Box Bottom" of flask-style boxes on page 12. Remember that this box has a ribbon hinge! Begin gluing in place at center fronts. Hold until dry. Continue to glue 1 leaf edge at a time, matching each score line with each point or dip of leaf. Butt INSIDE BOX SIDE'S finished edges up

to each other at center back. Emphasize leaf's shape by molding with fingers at wide parts of leaf and pinching at pointed parts of leaf.

Cut ⅝"-wide brown satin ribbon in half. Glue edge of each ribbon to wrong side of inside top edge of box, 1" from center back. Glue wrong side of OUTSIDE BOX SIDE to wrong side of INSIDE BOX SIDE. Begin gluing at center front. Match and glue 1 edge at a time, making sure glue is thoroughly flattened. Be careful to keep ribbon hinge extended out from box.

Press 2" x 5" strip of outer fabric from scraps into thirds lengthwise, hiding raw edges. Glue pressed strip over cardboard edges at center back, folding and gluing top and bottom tabs over to other side. Re-emphasize leaf's shape.

• Glue Ribbon Hinge to Inside Lid

Follow instructions for "Gluing Ribbon Hinge to Inside Lid" on page 12. Stitch ribbon hinges to MIDDLE LID, through cardboard, so ribbon hinges are attached closer to bottom edge of MIDDLE LID.

• Embellish Box

Turn box upside down. Glue edge of narrow antique gold metallic trim to underside edge of box bottom. Glue wrong side of BASE to bottom of box.

Embellish LID following instructions and diagram on page 119.

Tools and Materials

Heavy cardboard–18" x 36"
Lightweight cardboard–7" x 32"
Solid outer fabric (brown jacquard satin)–20" x 30", plus six different brown scraps of various textures and shades
Inside fabric (leaf print silk)–⅓ yd.
Quilt batting–¼ yd.
Iron-on fusing–10" square

¾ yd. each of 7 different trims
6" of ⅝"-wide brown satin ribbon
1 yd. narrow antique gold metallic trim
½ yd. each of ½"-wide purple, lavender and rose ribbon; matching thread
½ yd. of lt. green textured 7mm ribbon
1 yd. of ½"-wide dk. green textured ribbon
½ yd. black tiny picot trim
2 yds. ½"-wide lavender ribbon
½ yd. of 1½"-wide green wired ribbon
5 small, brown mother of pearl buttons

Hand sewing needle
1" and ½" wooden dowels

Heavy Cardboard	Light Cardboard	Inside Fabric	Outer Fabric
LID INSIDE BOTTOM INSIDE LID BASE and MIDDLE LID-cut 2	OUTSIDE BOX SIDE INSIDE BOX SIDE	INSIDE BOTTOM + ¾"* INSIDE LID + ¾"*	OUTSIDE BOX SIDE + 1"* INSIDE BOX SIDE + ¾"* LID + ¾"* BASE and MIDDLE LID + ½"* solid outer fabric-cut 2

* See page 8.

(A) Stitch 7 PANSIES with ½"-wide purple, lavender and rose ribbon. Mark intervals at ¼", 1½", 2", 1½" and ¼". Glue in place.

(B) Stitch 6 FOLDED LEAVES with lt. green textured 7mm ribbon. Glue in place. Hide raw edges under PANSIES.

(C) Tie a bow with ½"-wide dk. green textured ribbon. Glue in place. Drape tails and stitch in place with buttons at 1" intervals. Stitch bow loops down.

(D) Tie a small bow with black tiny picot trim. Glue in place in center of dk. green bow. Glue tail ends to underside of LID.

Turn LID upside down. FLUTE ½"-wide lavender ribbon while gluing onto underside of LID. Glue wrong side of LID to MIDDLE LID.

With 1½"-wide green wired ribbon, make a double bow and glue to inside center back of box.

OUTSIDE BOX SIDE and INSIDE BOX SIDE patterns reduced to 25% of original. Enlarge 400%.

All other patterns reduced to 50% of original. Enlarge 200%.

Placement Diagram.

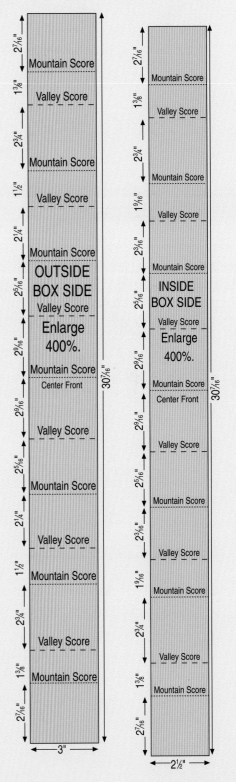

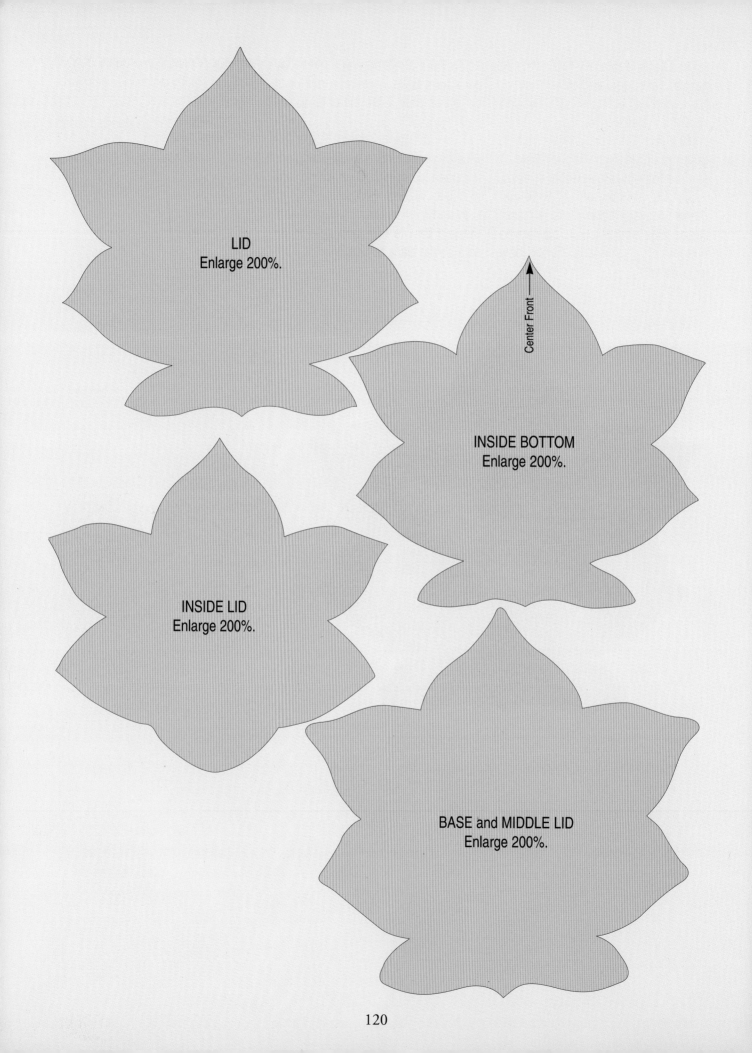

LID
Enlarge 200%.

Center Front

INSIDE BOTTOM
Enlarge 200%.

INSIDE LID
Enlarge 200%.

BASE and MIDDLE LID
Enlarge 200%.

Once in a Blue Moon

• *Cut Cardboard and Fabric, Score*

• *Cover Cardboard with Fabric and Shape*

Laminate 1 BASE with moon fabric and 1 BASE with accent fabric. Laminate 1 MIDDLE LID with outer fabric and 1 MIDDLE LID with accent fabric.

Laminate mountain-scored side of OUTSIDE BOX SIDE with outer fabric. Finish 2 long edges and 1 short edge. Place wrong side up on work surface. Fold at each mountain score and emphasize scores. Place right side up on work surface. Fold at each valley score and emphasize scores. Place OUTSIDE BOX SIDE wrong side up on work surface. Roll 19" length with 1" dowel. Turn over. Roll remaining length with 1" dowel for initial shaping. Use ½" and ¼" dowels to continue to shape edge to match INSIDE BOTTOM. Pinch box side at nose and mouth to accentuate features.

Laminate unscored side of INSIDE BOX SIDE with inside fabric. Finish all 4 edges. Place right side up on work surface. Roll 18⅛" length with 1" dowel. Turn over. Roll remaining length with 1" dowel.

Pad INSIDE BOTTOM with 1 layer of batting and wrap with inside fabric. Pad INSIDE LID with 3 layers of batting and wrap with inside fabric. Embroider LID before pad and wrap process.

• *Assemble Box Bottom*

Follow instructions for *"Assembling Box Bottom"* of hinge-lid-style boxes on page 12.

Carefully glue wrong side of INSIDE BOX SIDE with tacky glue and let set up for 2 minutes. Slip INSIDE BOTTOM into assembled box and glue in place. Mold and shape INSIDE BOX SIDE to OUTSIDE BOX SIDE. Hold in place with clothespins until dry. During drying time, continue to mold and pinch sides to shape.

Glue BASES wrong sides together. Glue gold side of combined BASE to bottom of box.

• *Assemble Lid*

Glue MIDDLE LIDS wrong sides together. Glue wrong side of INSIDE LID to velvet side of combined MIDDLE LID.

• *Embroider Lid and Finish Box*

Following stitch guide and chart on page 124, embroider LID fabric.
(A) Stitch brass charms in place.
(B) Stitch gold beads in place.

Pad LID with 1 layer of batting and wrap with moon fabric. Glue wrong side of LID to gold side of combined lid.

Tools and Materials
Heavy cardboard–20" x 30"
Lightweight cardboard–3" x 32"
Outer fabric (blue velvet)–¼ yd.
Accent fabric (gold lamé)–10" x 18"
Moon fabric (blue textured)–10" x 18"
Inside fabric (lt. blue and gold print)– ¼ yd.
Quilt batting–¼ yd.
Green/gold, and bright, lt., med., dk., and very dk. gold embroidery floss
3 "celestial" brass charms
5 gold beads
Size 3 crewel embroidery needle
Beading needle
Clothespins
1", ½" and ¼" dowels

Heavy Cardboard	Light Cardboard	Inside Fabric	Outer Fabric
INSIDE LID INSIDE BOTTOM and LID-cut 2 BASE and MIDDLE LID-cut 2	OUTSIDE BOX SIDE INSIDE BOX SIDE	INSIDE BOX SIDE + ¾"* INSIDE BOTTOM (facing right) + ¾"* INSIDE LID (facing left) + ¾"* **Accent Fabric** BASE (facing right) + ½"* MIDDLE LID (facing right) + ½"*	OUTSIDE BOX SIDE + ¾"* MIDDLE LID (facing left) + ½"* **Moon Fabric** BASE (facing left) + ½"* LID (facing left) + ¾"*

* See page 8.

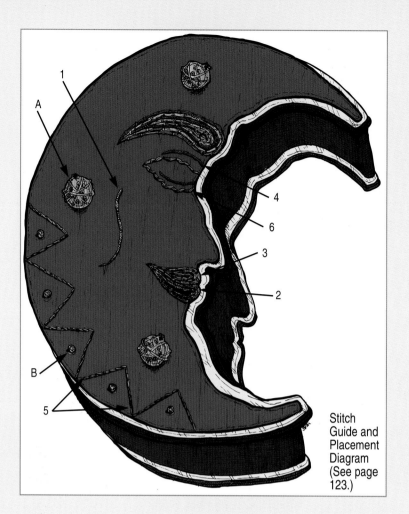

Stitch
Guide and
Placement
Diagram
(See page
123.)

#	*Stitch*	*Floss*
1	COUCHING STITCH	6 strands of lt. gold floss
2	COUCHING STITCH	6 strands of dk. gold floss
3	COUCHING STITCH	6 strands of med. gold floss
4	COUCHING STITCH	6 strands of very dk. gold floss
5	COUCHING STITCH	6 strands of bright gold floss
6	COUCHING STITCH	6 strands of green/gold floss

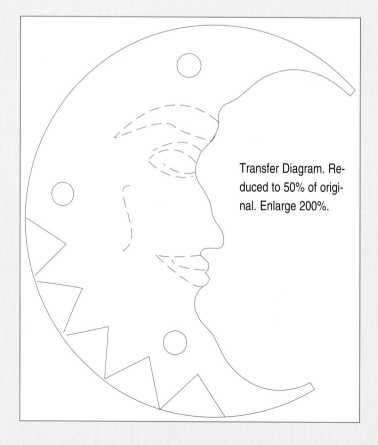

Transfer Diagram. Reduced to 50% of original. Enlarge 200%.

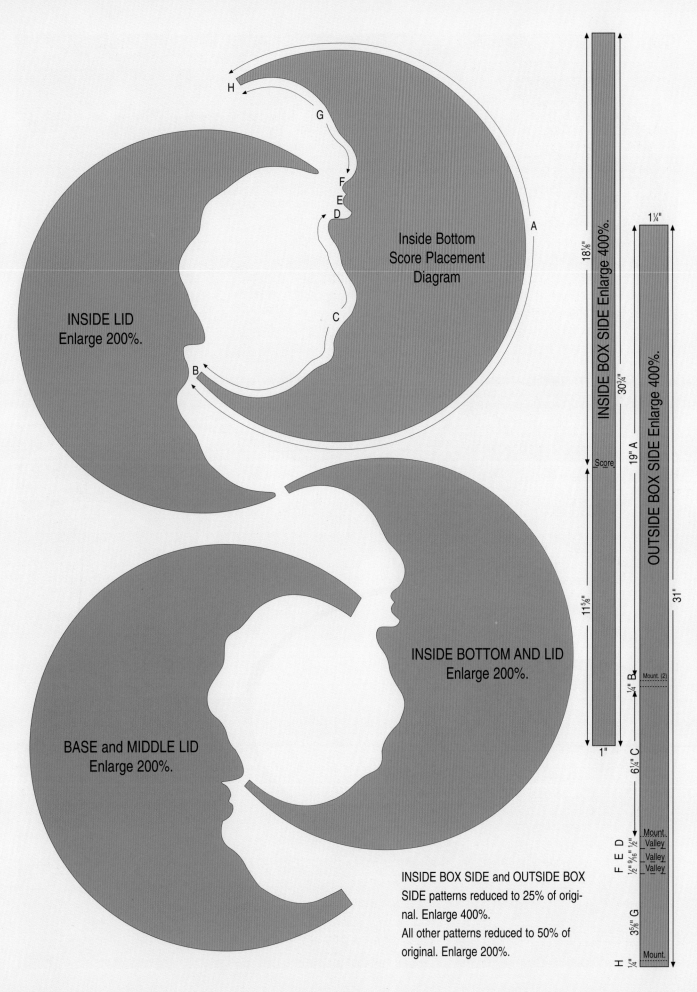

Inside Bottom
Score Placement
Diagram

INSIDE LID
Enlarge 200%.

INSIDE BOTTOM AND LID
Enlarge 200%.

BASE and MIDDLE LID
Enlarge 200%.

INSIDE BOX SIDE and OUTSIDE BOX
SIDE patterns reduced to 25% of original. Enlarge 400%.
All other patterns reduced to 50% of
original. Enlarge 200%.

INSIDE BOX SIDE Enlarge 400%.

OUTSIDE BOX SIDE Enlarge 400%.

18⅛"

30¾"

19" A

31"

11⅝"

Score

¼" B

Mount. (2)

1"

6¼" C

F E D

½" 9/16" ½"

Mount.
Valley
Valley
Valley

3⅝" G

Mount.

H
¼"

1¼"

Metric Equivalency Chart

MM-MILLIMETRES CM-CENTIMETRES
INCHES TO MILLIMETRES AND CENTIMETRES

INCHES	MM	CM	INCHES	CM	INCHES	CM
⅛	3	0.3	9	22.9	30	76.2
¼	6	0.6	10	25.4	31	78.7
½	13	1.3	12	30.5	33	83.8
⅝	16	1.6	13	33.0	34	86.4
¾	19	1.9	14	35.6	35	88.9
⅞	22	2.2	15	38.1	36	91.4
1	25	2.5	16	40.6	37	94.0
1¼	32	3.2	17	43.2	38	96.5
1½	38	3.8	18	45.7	39	99.1
1¾	44	4.4	19	48.3	40	101.6
2	51	5.1	20	50.8	41	104.1
2½	64	6.4	21	53.3	42	106.7
3	76	7.6	22	55.9	43	109.2
3½	89	8.9	23	58.4	44	111.8
4	102	10.2	24	61.0	45	114.3
4½	114	11.4	25	63.5	46	116.8
5	127	12.7	26	66.0	47	119.4
6	152	15.2	27	68.6	48	121.9
7	178	17.8	28	71.1	49	124.5
8	203	20.3	29	73.7	50	127.0

YARDS TO METRES

YARDS	METRES	YARDS	METRES	YARDS	METRES	YARDS	METRES	YARDS	METRES
⅛	0.11	2⅛	1.94	4⅛	3.77	6⅛	5.60	8⅛	7.43
¼	0.23	2¼	2.06	4¼	3.89	6¼	5.72	8¼	7.54
⅜	0.34	2⅜	2.17	4⅜	4.00	6⅜	5.83	8⅜	7.66
½	0.46	2½	2.29	4½	4.11	6½	5.94	8½	7.77
⅝	0.57	2⅝	2.40	4⅝	4.23	6⅝	6.06	8⅝	7.89
¾	0.69	2¾	2.51	4¾	4.34	6¾	6.17	8¾	8.00
⅞	0.80	2⅞	2.63	4⅞	4.46	6⅞	6.29	8⅞	8.12
1	0.91	3	2.74	5	4.57	7	6.40	9	8.23
1⅛	1.03	3⅛	2.86	5⅛	4.69	7⅛	6.52	9⅛	8.34
1¼	1.14	3¼	2.97	5¼	4.80	7¼	6.63	9¼	8.46
1⅜	1.26	3⅜	3.09	5⅜	4.91	7⅜	6.74	9⅜	8.57
1½	1.37	3½	3.20	5½	5.03	7½	6.86	9½	8.69
1⅝	1.49	3⅝	3.31	5⅝	5.14	7⅝	6.97	9⅝	8.80
1¾	1.60	3¾	3.43	5¾	5.26	7¾	7.09	9¾	8.92
1⅞	1.71	3⅞	3.54	5⅞	5.37	7⅞	7.20	9⅞	9.03
2	1.83	4	3.66	6	5.49	8	7.32	10	9.14

Index